The Secret Life of St Neots Station

A microcosm of the world it serves

John Slack

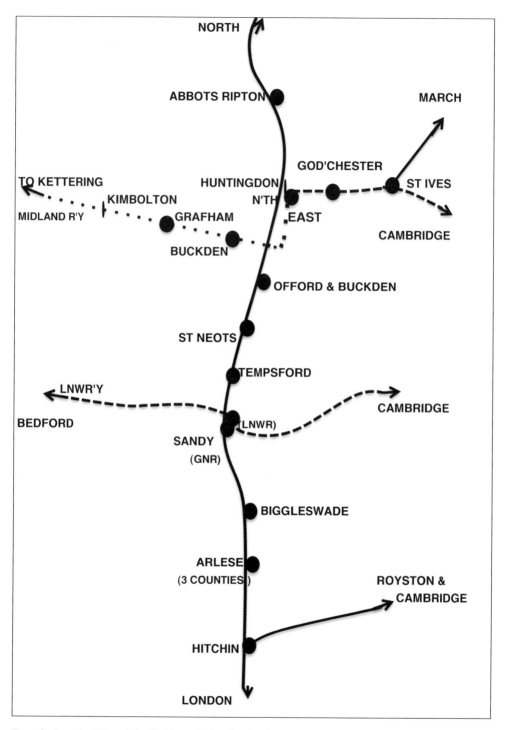

Frontispiece 1 – Map of the St. Neots Station local railway network (Drawn by Jenny Todd)

The Secret Life of St Neots Station

A microcosm of the world it serves

John Slack

Production by
Horizon Editions Ltd,
Trading as The Horizon Press
The Oaks, Moor Farm Road West, Ashbourne, DE6 1HD
Tel: (01335) 347349
books@thehorizonpress.co.uk

1st Edition
ISBN 978-1-84306-530-2

Print: Gomer Press, Llandysul, Ceredigion, Wales

Front cover: A busy early autumn scene in 1917 at the station dispatching hay and straw for the trenches on the Western Front. (Courtesy of David Bushby)

Back cover: 'Flying Scotsman' engine speeding through St. Neots Station in the snow in the 1950s. (Joe Doncaster collection)

Title page: Station footbridge sporting weather roof. (Joe Doncaster Collection)

Dedication
To my dear wife Dorothy for her support in this venture

Contents

Illustrations

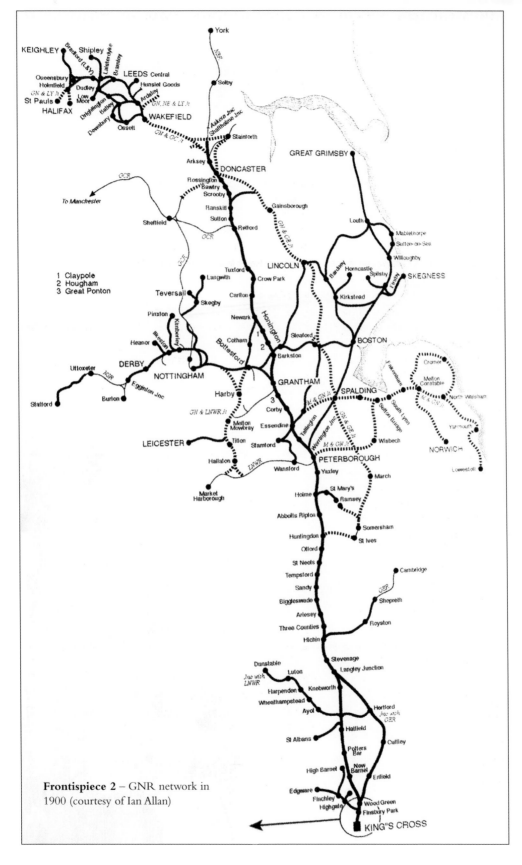

York
KEIGHLEY Shipley
Bradford (L&Y)
Queensbury Dudley Lanstercke Branley
Holmfield GN & LY Jr Low Drighlington LEEDS Central
St Pauls Moor Hunslet Goods
HALIFAX Batley Ardsley
Dewsbury Ossett GN, NE & LY Jr
Selby
WAKEFIELD
GN & GCR
Stainforth
GCR Arksey
To Manchester DONCASTER GREAT GRIMSBY
Rossington
Bawtry Gainsborough
Scrooby Louth
Sheffield Ranskill Mablethorpe
Sutton Retford Sutton-on-Sea
GCR GN & GE Jr Willoughby
1 Claypole GCR LINCOLN SKEGNESS
2 Hougham Tuxford Crow Park Bardney Horncastle
3 Great Ponton Langwith Spilsby
Teversall Carlton Kirkstead
Skegby Honington
Pinxton Newark Sleaford BOSTON
Heanor Ilkeston Kimberley Cotham Barkston
Uttoxeter Bottesford 1 Fakenham Melton Cromer
DERBY 2 GRANTHAM SPALDING Constable
Eggington Jnc NOTTINGHAM Barkston M & GN Jr North Walsham
Stafford Burton Harby SPALDING South Lynn
GN & LNWR Jr Corby Tollington Sutton Bridge M & GN Jr
3 Essendine Wernington Jnc GN & GE Jr Wisbech
LEICESTER Tilton Stamford PETERBOROUGH March NORWICH
Hallaton LNWR Wansford Yaxley Lowestoft
Market St Mary's
Harborough Holme Ramsey
Abbotts Ripton Somersham
Huntingdon St Ives
Offord
St Neots Cambridge
Tempsford
Sandy GER
Biggleswade Shepreth
Arlesey Royston
Three Counties
Hitchin
Dunstable Stevenage
Luton Langley Junction
Jnc with
LNWR Harpenden Knebworth
Wheathampstead Hertford
Ayot Jnc with
GER
Hatfield
St Albans Potters Cuffley
Bar
High Barnet New Enfield
Barnet
Edgware Finchley Wood Green
Highgate Finsbury Park
KING"S CROSS

Frontispiece 2 – GNR network in
1900 (courtesy of Ian Allan)

9

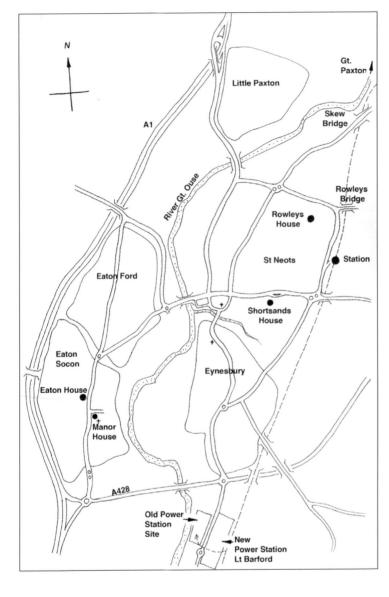

Frontispiece 3 – St. Neots map displaying some of the book's relevant features (Drawn by Paul Todd)

Abbreviations in the book

AGM - Annual General Meeting
BR – British Railways
BRB – British Railways Board
BTC – British Transport Commission
cwt – Hundredweight (20 = 1 ton)
d – Old penny (= 2.4 old pennies = 1 decimal penny)
s – shilling (1 = 5p, 20 = £1)
ft – foot/feet (3ft = 1 yard = 36" inches, 39.72" = 1 metre)

GNR – Great Northern Railway
L & NER – London & North Eastern Railway
LNWR – London & North Western Railway
MR – Midland Railway
NER – North Eastern Railway
S & DR - Stockton & Darlington Railway
Y & NMR – York & North Midland Railway

Acknowledgements

I am deeply indebted to the following people and institutions for their kind, empathetic help and approach they have offered to me during this project. The book crystallised in my mind when I discovered the existence of an album of unpublished award-winning local railway photographs taken over the period encompassing the late Forties to just before 1970 by a railway station employee called Joe Doncaster. His reminiscences of the period from the Thirties to the Sixties had also been taped. I felt these memories deserved to be aired for posterity.

As I am incarcerated in a wheelchair nowadays, this project's advance could not have occurred without the dedication of Barry Mills who willingly sacrificed his time to surf the local library's preserved newspapers dating from 1850 to 1984. He fed me with copious photocopies of relevant stories, often full of gory details with no-holds-barred.

I am indebted to Professor Paul Light who has selflessly given up his time to proof-read the draft copy. This project, designed to keep me 'off the streets and out of trouble', was supported by an incredibly large army of passionate railway buffs and historians all of whom fed me with photographs and information from their own archive material. I am merely the catalyst linking their input together into this thematic slice of history.

David Bushby, who is probably the most eminent of local historians, willingly agreed to allow me to use his copious information and photographs acquired over many decades. His legendary dedication into 'rooting out' long-lost important facts fits neatly into this account that has turned out to be a fully explanatory description of the social fabric and evolution of St. Neots during the Industrial Revolution.

Other friends who have helped enormously are Peter Hall, secretary of the Great Northern Railway Society. He was always there with ready information and contacts he knew who would get me out of 'tight corners', Jenny & Paul Todd and John Hall, superb computer boffins helping me, known as the "Frank Spencer" of the computer world, and Ian Hornsby who plied me with relevant books gleaned from shops I could not browse.

Other organisations and significant people who have played a part in donating illustrations and offering information from their specialist archival interests are:-

Dr. Mike Sharman, Linda Read, Anna Mercer (St. Neots Museum curator), Bob Burn-Murdock (Norris Museum curator, St Ives), Jake Duncombe, Sue Jarrett, Phyllis & Ken Barringer, Sam Malt, John Oxley, Allan Mott, Dorothy Slack, David Rudd, Judith Addington, Neville Cooper, Steven Todd, Andrew Rush, Allan Sibley (GNRS), Terry Henderson (GNRS), Hunts. Record Office, Nora Butler, St. Neots Reference Library, Dennis Tinley, and George Howe (Chairman GNRS).

I apologise in advance if anyone feels aggrieved at omission from the above list. All help has been very much appreciated.

The quality of some of the illustrations is considerably impaired due to their origins, age and original quality; for these reasons I apologise in advance.

Chapter One
Setting the Scene

Octavius Wilkinson was awakened by his alert valet at the unearthly hour of 4.30am on Wednesday morning. He had received a business letter the week before from Lincoln's Inn, London urging him to attend the Courts. Being a lawyer of note, after studying law in London, this was a job he must follow meticulously.

Octavius originated from Stokesley in North Yorkshire. His grandfather had been the mayor of Stockton-on-Tees and his brother was a close friend of George Stephenson and first chairman of the York to Darlington Railway Company. Octavius decided to set up a law firm in St Neots in 1830 despite the fact he had no family connections with the sleepy market town, twenty miles due west of Cambridge. His only knowledge of this market town was through his old Cambridge University friend Colonel William Peppercorn who invited Octavius, recently qualifying as a lawyer at Lincoln's Inn, to partner him in a proposed new law practice in the town.

Colonel Peppercorn was the local land agent for the Earl of Sandwich, the latter residing in grandiose splendour at Hinchingbrooke House, Huntingdon and who owned nearly half of central St. Neots at the time! The Colonel administered the rented properties.

Fig 1 – Eaton House, Octavius Wilkinson's mansion in Eaton Socon, St. Neots.
(Courtesy of Radio Links)

What was so special about today? Octavius liked a challenge. The Great North Road turnpike from the coach-stop Cock Inn, Eaton Socon was a mere one hundred yards from his mansion, and demanded seven hours of stamina-sapping and organ-shaking time to London. The smile on his lips, however, intimated that this journey was going to be different. He was going to head ten miles westward for Bedford Station (later to be known as "Bedford St. Johns") where his coachman would deposit him. This was the terminus of the branch from the main London-Birmingham line at Bletchley.

The line had been opened a few months before, in mid-1846 by the London & Birmingham Railway Company, under the meticulously careful attentions of the famous engineer Robert Stephenson. This was a chance to sample the new means of travel that was all the rage in the north of England. He was planning on doing the round trip in one day. Money was no object; his client was footing the bill, but the first class fare was a mighty 17 shillings return (85p – all refs. are today's value not taking into account inflation).

The 7.15am train to London was timetabled to arrive at 10.20am via Bletchley, and thus Octavius duly steamed into Euston Station, a fine monument to the new railway age and opened in 1837. Business concluded, the uneventful return on the 4pm train, taking only two and a half hours, saw him comfortably relaxed at home in front of a roaring fire with a glass of port in hand by nine o'clock in the evening. Job done in one day!

St. Neots was a slumberous market town on the eastern bank of the River Gt. Ouse. It stood on an east-west turnpike between Cambridge and Northampton that crossed the Great North Road turnpike a mere half mile to the west – in Eaton Socon. Travelling to London, or any other distant settlement, was an expedition and the market town's industries were disadvantaged by a lack of cheaper bulk transport facilities. There was a river trade by barge to and from King's Lynn but it was cumbersome.

Although the journey in the story so far is fictitious it gives you an idea of just how difficult travel was in those early Victorian years. Let us slip down the rabbit burrow of time and delve into a lost world of people's dreams, aspiration, stress, grief and many other facets of a human's lifetime of experiences.

Octavius, however, was a real person. His 'experience' of this new travel mode highlighted a malignant problem amongst coaching inns and the post-chaise operators on the Great North Road. Between 1837 and 1840 the first rail trunk route from hub-like York and the North to London had been opened up to Euston Station via Rotherham, Derby, Leicester and Rugby but it involved no less than three railway companies along its length.

The York to Derby companies' chairman and major shareholder, the contemporaneously-styled "King" George Hudson, was rubbing his podgy little hands with rapidly expanding wealth. This man appears at length during the 1840's in attempts

Bedford Railway Timetable December 1st 1846 (from Bradshaw's Guide)

Euston dep.	7.15 am	10.45 am	4.00 pm	5.30 pm
Bedford arr.	10.15 am	1.15 pm	6.30 pm	8.00 pm
Bedford dep.	7.15 am	10.00 am	2.10 pm	5.50 pm
Euston arr.	10.20 am	12.30 pm	5.00 pm	8.15 pm

to staunch other plans to wrestle this monopolistic position from his grasp. At last, a potential uninterrupted route to Scotland was showing signs of opening up.

Hudson, a York tailor's son, invested a family inheritance wisely in the York area by creating a railway network radiating out into Yorkshire and beyond. His greatest achievement, to date, and already mentioned, had been to create the first ever rail link between the North and London (Euston) via Derby and Rugby, and he was hell-bent on protecting this money-spinner that elevated

his national social standing to the point where he was invited to take tea with Queen Victoria.

This innovative trunk railway was an utter disaster for the coaching inns and their industry along the Great North Road. This new rail route came nowhere near this major road for people to seek alternative employment. Henry Walker, the landlord of the Cock Inn, Eaton Socon, a fine and vital 'oasis' for nomads and sited adjacent to the village church, filed for bankruptcy in 1845 citing the "merciless railroad" as

Fig 2 – George Hudson, self-styled 'King' of the railway industry at the height of his prime, with autograph and personal seal. (W. W. Tomlinson – 'History of NER Railway', 1912)

Fig 3 – Cock Inn, Eaton Socon in February 1845, family home of the Peppercorns 1845-1923 and renamed the 'Manor House'. (Courtesy - St. Neots Museum Collection)

the reason. The actual words used at the court proceedings were; "the misfortunes that have befallen him have arisen from no misconduct of his own, but simply from the sad reverses of his business occasioned by the establishment of the Rail Roads".

The Cock Inn was a fine place. It had three major bedrooms, one of which was called the 'Balloon Room'. Whatever went on there? It was well before the time when Mandy Rice-Davies went to ground nearby in the village during the infamous Christine Keeler Affair of the early 1960s! There were also three rooms for potential travellers waiting for transport. These rooms were called the 'London, York and Oxford Sitting Rooms' respectively detailing the tendrils of the coaching network from the village. After visiting Burleigh House, Princess Victoria had 'called in' two years before 1837 when she became Queen, presumably to eat and use the toilet facilities in a private room while horses were changed. William Turner, the artist, also used to frequent the Inn while travelling on commissions along the Great

North Road. He was not enamoured by the drinks which he described as "poisons"!

The auction of the Cock Inn's effects included over fifteen kilograms of plate, 160 tablecloths and forty featherbeds thus emphasising the grandeur of the Inn during its heyday. The freehold was mortgaged at £2,500 although this value had, by 1845, plummeted to £1,000 due to the shrinking commercial circumstances.

It was experiences like this, coupled with the knowledge that a new northern-aspiring railway from London had reached Cambridge and Ely (Eastern Counties Railway) in the same year as the Cock Inn's 1845 bankruptcy that finally tipped Walker over the edge. Derbyshire and Yorkshire coal was the goal for London merchants and this frightened the influential St. Neots businessmen and landowners. They realised there was a total danger of being by-passed and left to stagnate in a backwater of despair, seeing its very life blood as a market town drain away like a river at the end of a monsoon wet season.

Chapter Two
The Birth Pangs of the Great Northern Railway

Grandiose plans, which had to be confirmed by Acts of Parliament, were beginning to plough great iron-filled furrows northwards across undulating countryside from London. Anticipating tongues were beginning to wag in St Neots. Newspaper articles, such as in the "St Neots Chronicle", which kept locals informed of any 'whispers' of potential schemes emanating from the Capital.

The Wilkinson family had many connections with the well-established railway giants of the North East. In this world, more so then, it was who you knew that counted. Octavius had kept in close contact by letter with his family in that neck of the woods, and in particular with older brother George Hutton Wilkinson who appears on the scene, albeit briefly. George was born in Walsham Hall, Walsham-le-Willows, northern Suffolk just before the family moved back north, to Stokesley Manor, North Yorkshire where Octavius was born in 1806.

By the time the St. Neots' railway scene was bubbling with excitement in the early 1840s, George Wilkinson was living at Harperley Park near Bishop Auckland, south west Co. Durham. He was colluding with the great railway men such as George Stephenson.

George was an astute corporate gentleman who was chairman of the Bishop Auckland & Weardale , the York & Darlington, and Hartlepool Harbour & Railway companies. He also became a front-runner in support of a more direct London to York rail route. The first to appear was the London & York Company, in 1827 that followed a route

where the current railway is sited through St, Neots. Another company, the Direct Northern and a competitor to the former, showed a significant deviation around St. Neots by choosing a route along the River Gt. Ouse's flood plain on the opposite side of the river through Eaton Socon (and today's fine Riverside Park).

On May 18th 1844, after the formation of the final structure of the London & York, the company then agreed to join forces with the Doncaster-based Great Northern Railway and the latter name disappeared for the time being with the London & York Railway being adopted by the new corporate structure. A submission to the Board of Trade then led to the granting of an Act of Parliament to build the line through St. Neots along the line of the London & York route, and triggering the abandonment of the Direct Northern Eaton Socon route. This choice may well have brought a smile to the lips of Octavius Wilkinson because the Eaton Socon route would have been within a stone's throw of his garden.

By 1845, 20 years after the opening of the Stockton & Darlington Railway, the country was gripped in what was termed 'Railway Mania'. Steam engine technology had advanced rapidly. 1118 schemes, to build railways, popped up like wild mushrooms during that maniacal year (700 in November alone, the final submission date being the 30th). Most of them were thrown out by Parliament but not before shares had been sold and certificates issued.

George Wilkinson became a keen supporter

of the idea of a more direct railway out of London, through the St. Neots area, towards his beloved honey-pot area. Other supporters included Colonel Octavius Duncombe, MP for Yorkshire's North Riding but living at Waresley Park, eight miles south-east of St. Neots, and Francis Pym of The Hazells, Sandy, Bedfordshire. There was, however, a further competitor in the wings.

A Cambridge-Lincoln-Doncaster route plan, the structure of which was created by a Parliamentary Railway Committee and supported by "King" George Hudson, acted as catalysts together with a union of the two companies, the Cambridge & Lincoln (C & L, a subsidiary of the Eastern Counties) and the Direct Northern. The C & L would build north to Lincoln while the Direct Northern would complete this route to York, and abandon their plans through Eaton Socon from London. Skullduggery, claims, counter-claims and slander followed in the form of meetings in all the relevant towns and cities between London and York. What made matters worse for George Wilkinson was the fact that Hudson was the overall owner of the Wilkinson-led railway from York to Darlington!

Parliamentary approval for the Lincoln route left the London & York Railway, through St. Neots, with no future. The route's towns, including St. Neots, rose up in protest against this decision. Doncaster said that the "prosperity of the town was menaced". Bawtry accused the Board of Trade of "gross injustice". Biggleswade learnt of its decision "with deep regret and disappointment". Wakefield heard of it with "deepest concern".

On the other hand, the Mayor of Lincoln issued a puzzling statement passed by the City's Council supporting the London & York scheme. This immediately brought the population to a meeting at the cattle market between followers of the Cambridge & York and the more direct one through St. Neots. This 6,000-strong meeting broke up after the two sets of supporters resorted to stone-throwing, fighting and general disorder. It must have been quite a scene, a grander forerunner of such episodes associated with today's by-pass protests. The provision of a railway and station for St. Neots at that time was never more parlous.

Further confusion arose when support for a Cambridge-Peterborough-Doncaster extension came from the influential newspaper the Railway Times. Its sarcasm knew no bounds in its critical comments about the Direct Northern route plans through St. Neots with the following slur:

"Was it because the undertaking was not huge enough for public support that Cambridge, as a starting point, had been dropped – that seat of learned travellers deserted – the large traffic of taking students from the colleges removed from the table of estimates, and despised in comparison to proceeding direct to so celebrated and extensive a city as St. Neots (pop. less than 3,000 in 1841)? The public should next expect to hear that York Minster had been scheduled for removal to make room for a proper station".

Two more complications came on the scene. First, the aforementioned Eastern Counties Railway, having reached Ely, triggered off a plan to build a railway from that fine cathedral city to Huntingdon, St. Neots and Bedford in 1844 as the first east-west railway route to be met north of

London. Secondly, there was a Bill submitted to Parliament in the 1845 'Mania' rush to build a route by the Peterborough, St. Neots & Bedford Railway Company.

In January 1845 the Direct Northern Railway Company fired a warning shot across the bows by publishing a public notice comparing the route lengths, from London to York and Edinburgh, with the London & Birmingham, London & York, North Midland and Eastern Counties railways. The Direct Northern emphasised the fact that they were the shortest route (see fig. 8).

The eruption of all these possible routes north through St. Neots would have caused massive duplication of railway services along the Ouse Valley and, at the same time, turned St. Neots or Eaton Socon into a major railway junction town like Crewe or Clapham. All this potential competition caused the Ely company to withdraw the Huntingdon to Bedford section from their plans and concentrate on the Ely to Huntingdon part, which duly opened in 1847.

This is where Octavius Wilkinson appears once more. A letter was sent to him regarding the Ely & Bedford Railway Co. by its agents in King's Lynn (Goodwin, Partridge & Williams):–

"Lynn September 14th 1844
Dear Sir,

We send you a prospectus of the Ely & Bedford Railway and will send a packet as soon as we can obtain them. We have sent a prospectus to all the Provincial committee including the three Gentlemen of your Town. Our advertisements appear for the first time today, but the project has become known in Liverpool through our friend Mr. Lacy, and we have in consequence already received applications from substantial men up there for upwards of 2,000 shares.

Will you be kind enough to furnish us with particulars of all public carriages passing through St. Neots mentioning the number of passengers which the coaches are licensed to carry, whether the vans and the carriers carry passengers, and the class of goods carried etc. We send a prospectus to each of the gentlemen on the north side of the river upon whom we called the other day.

P.S. We are obliged by your letter respecting water traffic."

Fig 4 – Proposed Ely & Bedford Railway route map, via Eaton Ford, St. Neots 1844. (Courtesy of Huntingdon Record Office)

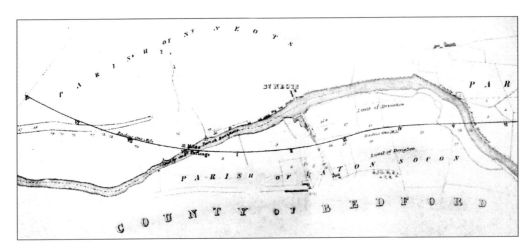

There was a fair amount of opposition to this Ely to Bedford scheme. If you study the illustrated map of the scheme it will be seen that the planned route would have cut across The Common as it approached St. Neots from the north. This involved the construction of an embankment along the length of this still magnificent open space that has acted as a major sporting centre for the past two centuries. A similar embankment would have been built through Eaton Socon along the line of the Direct Northern Railway's route before it bridged the river once more and away from Octavius Wilkinson's house.

Sam Day, the then clerk to the St. Neots Paving Commissioners, inspected the plans with the members and expressed the opinion that the route would be "most injurious to the town and tend permanently to flood it". It was proposed to call an informative

meeting of townsfolk and urge them to oppose the scheme. This was held at the beginning of January 1845, and resulted in a unanimous decision by the town to object to the plan. People power!

During the 1845 Mania period there was a proposal to build a 53-mile long railway from Cambridge, via Bourn, Great Gransden, Abbotsley, Eynesbury and Eaton Socon west to Souldrop (near Sharnbrook) and Northampton under the title The Midland & Eastern Counties Railway. It would have connected the Eastern Counties growing network with Rugby and onward to Manchester and Lancashire with its cotton industry.

Shares were offered to the public in 1845 but enthusiasm was lukewarm with ready money going into other more promising schemes. This fledgling company, however, was wound up the same year. This would

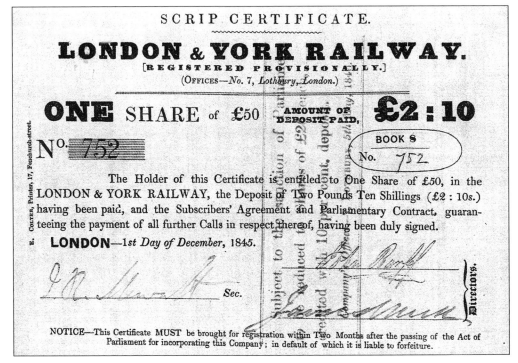

Fig 5 – London & York Railway Company share certificate. (Courtesy of Dr. Mike Sharman)

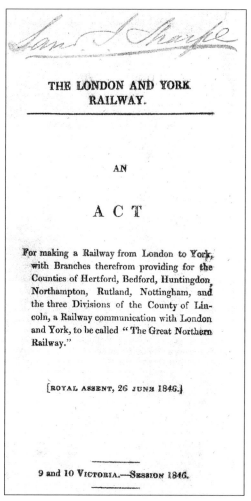

THE LONDON AND YORK
RAILWAY.

AN

A C T

For making a Railway from London to York,
with Branches therefrom providing for the
Counties of Hertford, Bedford, Huntingdon,
Northampton, Rutland, Nottingham, and
the three Divisions of the County of Lincoln, a Railway communication with London
and York, to be called "The Great Northern
Railway."

[ROYAL ASSENT, 26 JUNE 1846.]

9 and 10 VICTORIA.—SESSION 1846.

Fig 6 – Title page of London & York Act of
Parliament. (Courtesy of Dr. Mike Sharman)

have linked in with another contemporary
1845 scheme, the Rugby, Derby &
Manchester Railway but even that failed
due to its duplication of routes already
established.

If the Cambridge to Northampton scheme
had come to fruition this would have created
a railway junction either in Eynesbury (a
southern suburb of St. Neots) or Eaton
Socon (a western suburb of the town).
The Midland & Eastern Counties surveyor
planned a junction for both north-seeking
railway schemes because no decision had

been made as to which one was to be built
at that time. (If only this east-west route had
been built; it would be worth its weight in
gold today to relieve the A14 trunk road of
its Felixstowe container traffic.)

If the surveyor's map of the Midland &
Eastern Counties' route through St. Neots
(Eaton Socon and Eynesbury) is studied, it
can be seen that there is a dashed line about
170 yards on each side of the proposed east-
west route. This was the adjustment distance
(or "Deviation") allowed by Government
in all surveys of potential railway schemes
to allow for any unforeseen geological and
landscape problems that may surface during
construction.

This came into usage when a certain
prominent St. Neots landowner, one
George William Rowley entered the fray
to create his own, as some people might
say, avaricious financial demands (to be
discussed in the next section). Little wonder
that some of the great railway builders of
the time enjoyed such perilously short lives
with all the 'flak' that was thrown at them.

The whole process, of establishing the
basis of a parliamentary bill, turned out
to be the greatest corporate battle in the
history of British railway building. The saga
even involved calling for the revered advice
of three of the greatest ever iconic figures in
the growth of the World's railways, Robert
Stephenson, Isombard Kingdom Brunel,
and Sir Joseph Pease MP (son of Edward,
'Father of the Railways' and saviour of the
Stockton & Darlington Railway with a last
minute £7,000 mortgage offer to save that,
and the future of railways). The process was
often on a knife-edge with the plans swaying
in favour of Bishopsgate (now Liverpool
Street) to Cambridge one week then to
King's Cross the next. The 'birth' eventually

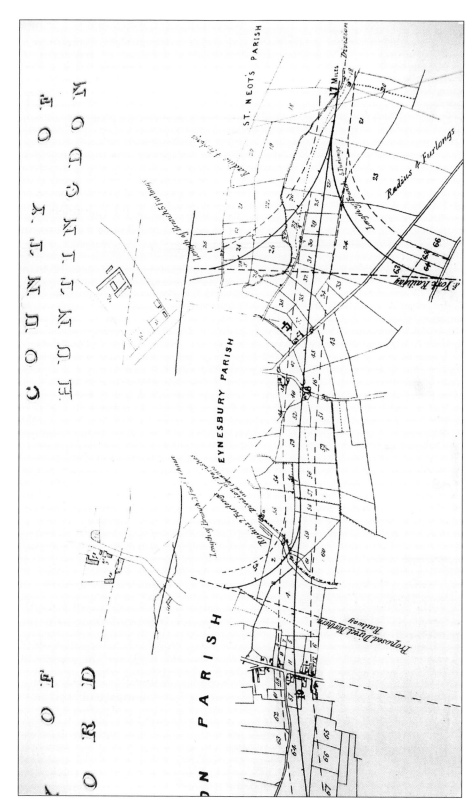

Fig 7 – Midland & Eastern Counties Railway map showing proposed junctions at Eynesbury and Eaton Socon with London & York and Direct Northern Railways, 1845. (Courtesy of Bedford Record Office)

DIRECT NORTHERN RAILWAY

FROM

LONDON TO YORK BY LINCOLN.

	Miles.
London to Manchester as at present, ...	$197\frac{1}{2}$
Saving by Churnet Valley, ...	23
	$174\frac{1}{2}$
Manchester to Carlisle by Bolton and Preston, ...	$121\frac{1}{2}$
	296
Carlisle to Edinburgh by Caledonian, ...	100
London to Edinburgh via Carlisle, ...	396

London to York by existing Line by Derby, ...	219	
York to Edinburgh by East Coast Lines	203	
		422

Making the Caledonian the shortest Way to London, over present }
    Lines, by . . . . }   26

If the Direct Northern Line is adopted from London to York the distance
will then be thus :—

	Miles.
London to York by Direct Northern, ...	$176\frac{1}{4}$
York to Edinburgh by East Coast, ...	203
	$379\frac{1}{4}$
Edinburgh to London by Caledonian, ...	396
	$16\frac{3}{4}$

Making the East Coast Lines the shortest by $16\frac{3}{4}$ miles, in connexion with
the Direct Northern.

If the London and York is adopted.

London to York by London and York, ...	186
York to Edinburgh, ...	203
	389
Edinburgh to London by Caledonian, ...	396
	7

    A difference nearly of 7 miles, just enough to secure a ruinous competition for the
traffic which the $16\frac{3}{4}$ saved by the Direct Northern prevent.

January, 1845.

Fig 8 – Direct Northern Railway London to York mileage sheet comparing alternative routes of other
companies to York and Edinburgh. Printed in January, 1845.

Fig 9 – Surveying party at work along the proposed route. (Source – C.H. Grinling)

needed that 'knife' for the equivalent of a Caesarian operation for the latter terminus to succeed, and this is how it came about.

The very future of a railway station at St. Neots hung in the balance from the 'Mania' guillotine date of November 30th 1845 until the birth of the G.N.R. at the end of June just over six months later.

The extremely complex picture of building plans of the London & York, Eastern Counties Extension (C & L), and Direct Northern meant there were three rival lines beaming in on York from London and only one was going to be given the nod by the Board of Trade as an Act of Parliament. The Eastern Counties Extension would own the more easterly route from London and Cambridge to Lincoln and the Direct Northern would take over from there to York, possibly missing out Doncaster. The London & York (L & Y), however, would 'cock-a-snoot' at 'King' Hudson and be the more direct line along the present East Coast Main Line.

'King' Hudson tried to trigger an abortion of the King's Cross to Doncaster route by offering the Direct Northern an "amalgamation" deal but the terms were so biased that it was viewed as a takeover bid by the back door. The man really did not have many scruples. The Direct Northern must have been ahead of the game because, while it toyed with the amalgamation idea for the first few months of 1846, the sly directors made overtures to the London & York!

The Board of Trade committee battles in London in the first half of 1846 were remarkably vicious affairs, and it was at this point that the expertise and wise counsel of Stephenson, Brunel and Pease were solicited. The details can be studied in Charles Grinling's 1898 book on the history of the Great Northern Railway but are not the catalyst for this book; that was Joe Doncaster who you will 'meet' in the middle of the next century later in the book.

Eventually, the dust began to settle to lay the foundations of the London & York and Direct Northern amalgamation, and 'King' Hudson was left to lick his wounds. His northern railway empire was also under attack from another direction, this time from Manchester, Sheffield, Leeds and Grimsby.

The 'Mania' was erupting all around him thus influencing him to illegally 'wheeler-deal' in his company shares and attracting the attentions of Mr. Prance of the London Stock Exchange in 1849. In turn, this led to the subtle but fatal blow that triggered Hudson's 'abdication'.

The combined cash funds won the day. The total was accumulated by the amalgamation of the London & York (£115,000) and the surprisingly healthier Direct Northern (£335,000) companies' remaining resources from invested deposits for shares by subscribers. The former's name was adopted for the new corporate title but only for a few months before the Great Northern Railway's name was adopted for the Parliamentary Bill.

Where did the name "Great Northern Railway" originate? This company already existed, and it was growing southwards out of Doncaster towards Lincoln, Boston and Peterborough. Prior to this, the first G.N.R. line to be opened, on April 1st, 1848, was between Louth, Grimsby and New Holland (on the Humber) with the 'Loop Line', via Lincoln and Boston to Peterborough a close second. London to Peterborough via St. Neots was to be a close third.

The Act of Parliament granting permission for the Great Northern Railway (G.N.R.) to commence building was passed on the 26th June 1846. The Act allowed the G.N.R. to raise £5,600,000 (£3 billion today – one quarter of the Channel Tunnel's cost) of capital for the scheme's completed 285.25 miles of track, both records for the time. The money was to be raised by a share offer and mortgage deals, and was the biggest scheme so far in the United Kingdom.

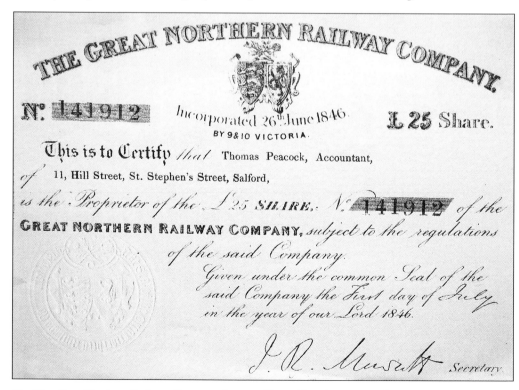

Fig 10 – Great Northern Railway Company share certificate 1846. (Source – author)

The Line that William Built and the Frustrations of a Local NIMBY

The surveyors and directors of the companies that planned the first few decades of railway building were plagued beyond measure by attempts of local landowners to either divert them from their estates or attract them towards their environs for personal use and financial self-interests. Some were successful due to their hierarchical position in the House of Lords, but George William Rowley was no lord. His estate and country house were an eastern mile beyond the edge of St. Neots at the top end of what is today known as Priory Park, a glorious green lung public open space.

The earlier comment stating that local influential landowners often possessed the ability to alter a projected railway's route has settled into St. Neots folklore over the physical position of the G.N.R. past the town. The fable that Mr. Rowley was directly responsible for the station being sited so far away from the town centre (one mile) could not be further from the truth. The station was built in the very last place he wanted it, within a stone's throw of his country retreat, and on the very edge of his park!

George William had grandiose designs on expanding Priory Park to the east, extending the house to create a large mansion, and thus establishing himself as a major country gentleman. His sister had left him £3,000 in 1838 to help towards this plan, and architectural drawings had already been committed to paper when the threat of the London & York Railway cutting through the expanded estate erupted in the early 1840s. Any further expansion by him eastwards was put on hold. More steam from ears episodes!

This frustrated man may well have been St. Neots' original NIMBY ('Not In My Back Yard'), and he expressed his attitude very clearly with the plain and unashamed statement: "Go where you please, go as conveniently as you can for the public, but leave me alone." As early as August 3rd 1844 he had written to the London & York Company suggesting the line should avoid his estate and pass through Eaton Socon and Hail Weston village.

Mr. Rowley claimed that the Eaton Socon route would "meet the general concurrence of the landed proprietors of Huntingdonshire". He had gone so far as to join the provisional committee of the London & York Company and even offered to become a shareholder investing as much as £5,000 if they would accede to his wishes. When he realised this string-pulling was not going to work he wrote to the then chief engineer, William Cubitt, suggesting that the station should be built on the side of the line furthest from St. Neots. I presume that "the line" was the most easterly dashed line of deviation allowed by Government legislation to be built into the railway surveyor's mandate (and commented on earlier). This was turned down out of hand.

Not only was George William concerned that the projected line would run within a few hundred yards of his house, he also feared that people going to the station would want to use the footpath through his estate. He was also concerned as to how near the houses that were to be built for the construction workers of the line would be to his own Priory House.

In the end, like many issues overseen by the Company's 'father' and first chairman Edmund Denison, it became one of compensation, and George William expected this to be substantial. When he was offered £8,000 plus an unstated extra amount for any damage and nuisance that might be caused, he turned up his nose and described it as "a miserable sum". He also saw it as a further proof that, although the railway would benefit people and the town, "the Leviathan Company", as he described it, was concerned only with its own profits.

Initially, George William intimated he would accept £12,500, but later withdrew that and pushed out the boat for £15,000! The affair rumbled on at its own pace and was not settled until after the railway had been opened. The Company refused to budge an inch on its original offer, so the matter had to go before a jury. On the first Saturday in November 1847 a jury was empanelled and, under the presidency of George Game, the Under-sheriff of Huntingdonshire, considered the evidence.

Mr. Rowley had engaged no less an expert than the Attorney General to represent him, while the Company was fronted by John Stuart Wortley MP. A variety of witnesses gave evidence on the value of the land, the quality of Rowley's estate, and other similar matters. In the final deliberation the jury decided the amount of compensation should be (yes, you've guessed it) £8,000! George William was left well out of pocket after this self-interested adventure to the courts in his attempt to get the better of the Great Northern.

George William was not the only landowner to be treated roughly by the Company. The Lord of Eynesbury Manor (at this time still a separate area from St. Neots), Captain William Humbley was also notified that his land was required and he parted with this to the Company in early 1846. By March 1848, however, he

had still received no payment, and to add insult to injury, found that the Company had disposed of the unwanted land within the dashed lines to his neighbour, George William Rowley, who, in turn, had absorbed it into his land and was growing crops on it! Only the strongest representations produced a satisfactory response from the Company in favour of Captain Humbley.

There was one other, fairly local, person who would have been keeping a close eye on this intriguing 'battle', and he was the Honourable Octavius Duncombe of Waresley Hall. He originated from Helmsley Park, South-west North Yorkshire Moors and had been the Member of Parliament for the North Riding of Yorkshire since 1841 when he was 24 years of age. He became a founder director of the G.N.R. in 1846 along with 47 other able bodies.

He took leave of absence from this task in 1850 until 1858 during which time he pursued his duties in Westminster and administering his estates in Waresley and Helmsley, the latter being at the north-west end of the Vale of Pickering. A second stint as a director then followed, for six years, from 1858 until he was elevated to Deputy Chairman for a further four years (in conjunction with three other deputies).

When the chairmanship became vacant in 1874 he was elevated for a second, and final, time to the illustrious post of full Chairman. This post he held for nearly six years, from 1874 to 1879. In that period he oversaw the extension of the company westwards to Stafford from Nottingham thus enabling the G.N.R. to exploit the quality coal of the highly productive East Derbyshire-West Nottinghamshire Coalfield which was based on the Leen, Erewash and Heanor valleys. The coke-hungry blast furnaces at Stanton, close to the south of Ilkeston, were linked by a branch to the company's main line.

The G.N.R. network stretched from King's Cross (with running rights to Crystal Palace, Dover and Clapham Junction) north to Lincoln, Grimsby, Doncaster, Leeds, Bradford, Shipley, Derby and Stafford. Running rights extended this spider's web to Manchester from where a third share of a joint company entitled the Cheshire Lines Committee allowed direct access to Chester, Liverpool and Southport and, with a half share in a line with the Great Western Railway, to Birkenhead in the Wirral Peninsula.

The Midland & Gt. Northern Railway was added a decade later, stretching the G.N.R.'s influence to Great Yarmouth and Lowestoft (Norfolk & Suffolk Joint Railway)

Fig 11 – Octavius Duncombe of Waresley. Painting at Helmsley Park, possibly a unique image. Chairman of the G.N.R. 1874-79.
(By kind permission of Feversham Settled Estates' Trustees. Photo by Jake Duncombe)

The Building of the Railway through St. Neots

Once the Act had been granted by Parliament in June 1846, moves to construct the line pressed ahead rapidly. The contract to build was offered to Thomas Brassey, a nationally renowned civil contractor, educated at Rugby School and Oxford University, due to his quality estimate being substantially lower than his rivals.

Thomas Brassey's large and, at the time, famous company was not only noted for the excellent quality of its work, but also had the necessary organisation and resources to undertake the full King's Cross to Doncaster operation which, to date, will have been the greatest railway project ever to be constructed in the U.K.

The work was sub-contracted, but Brassey supplied the tools and plant that were needed. This worked well, although there were some cases of workers having to sue sub-contractors in the local courts to obtain payment of their wages. No doubt this was all due to tightness of money right from the top office of the G.N.R.

The cost of the whole operation was so great with the majority of the cash coming from bank mortgages. This meant money was leaking out in all directions and no earnings to top up the account. The whole financial scene must have been a juggling nightmare for those involved but it did not help the navvies trying to exist on bread, cheese, pickled onions and the 'occasional' pint of beer.

Thomas Brassey himself kept a careful eye on the construction work at all stages by visiting the various sites every two to three months. However, progress could only happen during good weather and had to be shut down almost completely during the worst of the winter months. A diligent hard-worker, Brassey was probably the most eminent and underrated contractor of his age. He was responsible for one mile of construction in every three in the U.K. during his working life plus a near-matching record abroad.

Fig 12 – Thomas Brassey in 1865.
(Source - Internet)

Advantage would always be taken of any spell of good weather, and it was reported in early December 1847 that some of the men who had been discharged the previous week had been taken on again because the return of favourable weather meant that excavations could resume. There was no unemployment benefit in those days and, with no money coming into the house, cold wet weather conditions must have been dire. No wonder there were spells of occasional ill-health sweeping through the temporary camps.

Conditions were not so favourable in 1848 and, by the beginning of December,

work had almost stopped completely for the winter after a summer of less progress than had been anticipated. Although the official first sod had been dug in 1846 it was May 1849 before there was much evidence of work being carried out in the St. Neots area. Navvies began to shift earth to level out several small hills such as Priory and Paxton Hills with deep cuttings.

This St. Neots stretch of line was sub-contracted to three people. Little Barford to Eynesbury was the responsibility of William Swift; the next northward stretch, through Priory Hill to Paxton Hill went to William Wetherall, while Thomas Matthews carried the work from Great Paxton to Offord.

Some of the men in charge knew how to take (legal) advantage of the sudden increase in the population close to the line excavations. Samuel Radcliffe began working for Wetherall in December 1847 at the age of eighteen and stayed the pace until completion of the line in the summer of 1850.

Radcliffe's foreman ganger was John Haynes, son-in-law of the boss William Wetherall, and first landlord of the recently-erected Railway Tavern James Paine Brewery public house (later to be re-named the Engine & Tender). This pub was situated close to the station approach and the Cambridge Road railway bridge.

It appears later in this story, in World War Two, and was also the home, in the 1960s, of John Gregory the England football player and the Aston Villa manager in the last ever Cup Final at the old Wembley Stadium in 2000. This pub was one of at least five in the locality where the horses used on the construction work were stabled. Another was the Peacock Inn, not a stone's throw away. It will also appear in a later, somewhat

Fig 13 – Railway cutting excavation before the advent of modern machinery.
(Source – 'The Iron Road')

Fig 14 – Railway embankment construction, 1845, before today's heavy machinery.
(Source – C.H. Grinling)

Fig 15 – Interior of a Navvy family's hut, 1850. (Source – Internet)

gruesome, railway story and still stands as a white-washed derelict reminder of yesteryear. The Engine and Tender was demolished in the 1980s.

Samuel Radcliffe recalled Thomas Brassey's regular visits to inspect the works. A true railway-man, Brassey would take the train, on one of the lines already described, to Cambridge or Bedford and then travel by road to St. Neots where he would reside at the Cross Keys Hotel in the Market Square. An early riser, he would be up at the works at first light where he would talk to both the foremen and the labourers. He not only had a remarkable memory for names and faces, but also possessed the happy knack of being able to put himself alongside the workforce and talk easily with them.

Construction gangs of navvies, fuelled by the 'drop-down liquid' called beer, often spread great forebodings amongst local natives but there appeared to have been remarkably little trouble in the neigh-bourhood, except for a certain amount of poaching. In scarce money times, especially when the men were laid off in winter, the only available meat was a rabbit. They were still the preserve of the landowners and were jealously guarded by draconian laws and devious gamekeepers.

In October 1849, six navvies were caught poaching on the Croxton Park estate of Lord Eltisley and were sentenced to a fine of £2/10/0d each (£2.50) or two months in the County gaol with hard labour, this being the standard penalty. The general testimony, however, was one of good order and industry, and there was a genuine sense of co-operation between the railway workers and the townspeople.

In the year 2008 the unique archaeological excavation of a navvies' camp was conducted by television's Channel 4 "Time Team" at Risehill Tunnel on the Settle to Carlisle line. This fascinating delve into the past showed that the construction gangs were composed of 60% men, 25% children and 15% women! The navvies lived in huts and, if the men had wives and children accompanying them, these social units had a hut to themselves.

Where this temporary village was situated in St. Neots is not known.

At Christmas 1849, Harvey's, the brick and stonework sub-contractor to the railway company, joined forces with local merchants, who had fared well out of the extra trade, to lay on a fine festive meal. It was felt that great credit was due to the contractors "for the manner they rule their men" as they had caused no trouble in the neighbourhood.

The local press contained regular reports of the progress of construction. It wasn't until February 1850 that station building was going to start. By the beginning of June, just two months before the official opening of the line, ballast arrived to lay the foundations for permanent rails, and the end of the month saw the station and the iron bridge over Cambridge Road nearly completed. There was a tight race against time!

With the labour intensive nature of the job in those days, and health & safety being a phrase not yet in the English language, it was inevitable that there would be some accidents. In January 1850 a navvy was killed near St. Neots when a bank of earth collapsed on top of him. In April, another workman had to have his foot amputated after he slipped while attempting to climb onto an engine's tender bringing ballast from Sandy to Little Barford and the rear wheel flattened his metatarsals.

The line's construction, as was almost inevitable with so ambitious a scheme, had fallen behind schedule. The original completion date had been June 1st 1849 but the grand opening was postponed to the following August. It was with the most acceptable excuse that this London to Peterborough section of the G.N.R. was the longest stretch of line in the country to be opened in one fell swoop in the U.K.

St. Neots people would have seen the contractors' engines at work, but their first taste of passenger traffic was on Monday July 15th 1850. On that day, an engine with two carriages transported the project's chief engineer William Cubitt and others the full length of the line to inspect the work with the station buildings at St. Neots, erected by William Parker, drawing great praise. Job done just in time!

On the evening of August 7th, the day before the official opening of the railway and St. Neots Station, there were two celebration meals, one for more than 300 of the navvies, and the other for a further 200 of them. Mr. Culshaw, Company works superintendent, was present and "took a most anxious step for the comfort of one and all present". A band of music was engaged and it was the greatest pleasure to witness the friendly feeling that existed between master and men".

A later second meal, a supper, was arranged at the suggestion of the Commissioners' clerk, Samuel Day, and it was paid for by a subscription raised by the townsfolk. Several toasts and speeches were offered, of varying quality, from both railway workers and responded to by locals. It was described as: "After ample justice had been done to the liberal fare, the usual toasts were drunk, and many of them responded to with much propriety by the men themselves. Several gentleman present bore testimony to their good conduct and civil bearing from the commencement of the works. The party separated quietly at 10 o'clock much pleased with their evening's entertainment." So, no legends of alcoholic riots and pillage during the construction entered into local folklore.

Chapter Three
The Glory Days of the Great Northern Railway

The Grand Opening Day Arrives

On Monday August 5th, two days before the official opening of the new London to Peterborough line, the directors had ordered a train of two engines and seventeen carriages to 'try out the line'. The following account of this inspection run, written by an invited journalist from the contemporary London Illustrated News, sets this exciting and vibrant scene perfectly: "The line from Maiden Lane to Peterborough had been certified by the Government inspectors to be fit for traffic. On Monday, in order to further the test of its efficiency, the Contractors (Thomas Brassey) invited the Directors to take a trip down the line and satisfy themselves as to the manner in which the work had been performed.

Fig 16 – G.N.R. inspection train on its first run on August 5th 1850.
(Source – Grinling's History of the GNR, 1888)

At 9 o'clock, a party of about 400 gentlemen, filling altogether 17 carriages, took their departure from Maiden Lane. The equipment and general appearance of the train was peculiar. The carriages were all built of teak, by Mr. Williams of Goswell Street, and instead of being painted, the wood grain is polished and highly varnished, by which a great economy is effected both in time and expense of construction.

The internal fittings are of much the same character; the first class carriages being quite as comfortable though perhaps less showy than those on other lines, and the second and third being vastly better than anything of the same stamp.

The train quickly steamed into open countryside and passed through several stations, in various states of construction, to a late morning non-stopping show at St. Neots 53 miles to the north. The station's two platforms and buildings were bedecked

with flags, bunting and spectators where special platform tickets were issued for the day.

On to Peterborough for one o'clock where, with salivating mouths, the travellers were disgorged onto Peterborough North Station and were joined by Edmund Denison MP, the G.N.R. company chairman who had travelled down from the Doncaster headquarters via the new Lincoln to Boston Loop-line. He couldn't resist the thought of the magnificence of the occasion and the exposure of such an occasion that would do his political career no harm.

Fig 17 – Sir Edmund Denison, first chairman of the G.N.R. (Source – C. H. Grinling)

The party of selected guests sat down to a "very elegant dejeuner" laid out in the station supplied by Mr. Binney of the Crown Hotel. The feasters were joined by a large number of directors and officials of other companies.

On the return journey the new Company

Locomotive Superintendent, Archibald Sturrock, took over the driver's position in Peterborough and, at some point nearer to London, ran into the back of a works' engine out with a gang of navvies titivating the line-side earthworks. This was surely the first accident involving a moving passenger train on the new line."

The day after, on August 6th, Queen Victoria, accompanied by Prince Albert, inspected the new line through St. Neots. She nearly aborted the journey at the official opening of the famous Welwyn Viaduct when she refused to cross because it frightened her so much. The day was rescued when she descended to road level, entered a coach and travelled on the ground to the northern end and proceeded north.

The official opening of St. Neots Station itself occurred on Wednesday August 7th 1850. The G.N.R. issued platform tickets to the gathering crowd as a means of number control, and the tickets were supposed to have been handed in to the clerk after the event. At least one was 'forgotten', hence the current existence of this illustration.

The occasion was regarded by the town as being so important nearly all the shops closed so that everyone had the chance to visit the garlanded station. General public trains for the rest of August were used well and were known as 'Parliamentaries' (or 'Parleys') because that auspicious political body had decreed that, so as to save travellers from being overcharged and allow people to use them to pass to and from a place of work, at least one train a day in each direction must stop at every station and halt, and charge no more than a penny a mile.

Such was the success of this new trunk line it attracted the travelling attendance of a certain 'King' George Hudson who

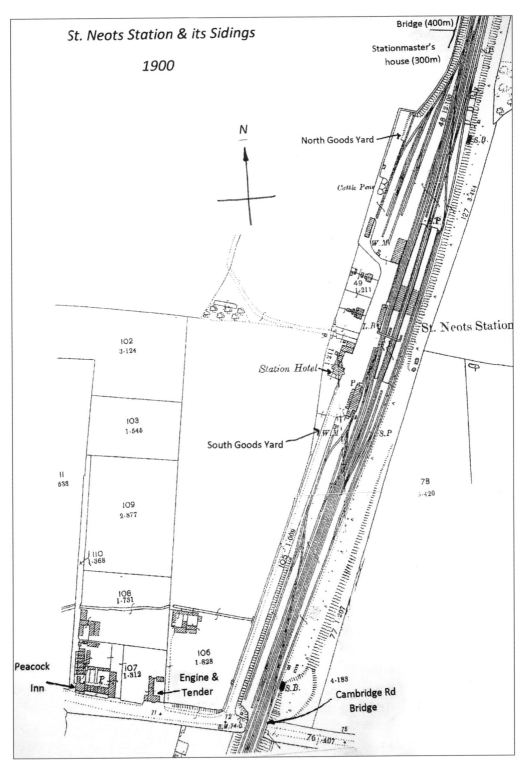

Fig 18 – Map of St. Neots Station in 1900 showing the North and South goods yards.
(Courtesy of Huntingdon Record Office)

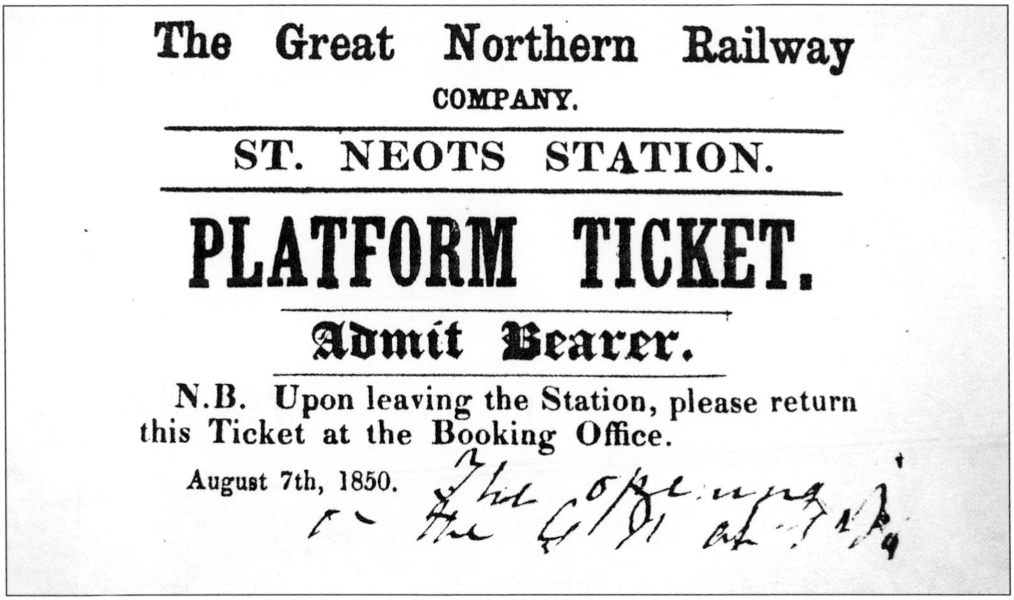

The Great Northern Railway
COMPANY.

ST. NEOTS STATION.

PLATFORM TICKET.

Admit Bearer.

N.B. Upon leaving the Station, please return
this Ticket at the Booking Office.

August 7th, 1850.

Fig 19 – St. Neots Station platform ticket for the grand opening of the line, August 7th 1850.
(Courtesy of Huntingdon Record Office)

was observed taking a seat in a first-class compartment at Maiden Lane just nine days after the opening! He was acting as an ordinary traveller for Leeds – via Peterborough, Boston, Lincoln, Gainsborough and Doncaster! The sly devil was 'tasting the competition' to his Euston, Rugby, Derby, Rotherham route.

A commentator said, "Here was Nemesis indeed. It was as if Jack's giant, instead of being killed outright, had shrunk to common size and then used Jack's beanstalk to come down to live with men. The George Hudson who surveyed from the windows of that Great Northern carriage the monarchy that had been his was now merely magni nominis umbra" (a ghost of his former eminence). When he arrived at Leeds he was heard to utter a few words of praise of the excellence of the journey. When he left the station, and realising a new era had dawned, he also passed out of the history of British railways.

Returning to the humble buildings of St. Neots Station, and while the opening day's euphoria was still bubbling, day excursions were provided for people to travel as far as London or closer to home for a day at Huntingdon Races. Such was the demand for tickets for a 12.35pm 'Special' to the more popular day out to Huntingdon, that a Tokyo Underground rush-hour type crush developed trying to board the train. A second train was steamed and dispatched from Huntingdon Station to satisfy the demand but by the time it arrived many prospective punters had given up and gone home. This was the only blot on what was otherwise one of the most significant days in the more modern history of St. Neots.

The town station of 1850 was a very simple structure and the public was offered few amenities to passengers. At this stage, throughout the Company's system, there were just two lines, an 'Up line' (to London) and a 'Down line' northwards. All traffic,

Fig 20 – St. Neots Station scene on the opening day
August 7th 1850.
(Kind permission of Huntingdon Record Office)

The First-Class Passenger   The Second-Class Passenger   The Third-Class Passenger

Fig 21 – Contemporary compartments depicting the 3 classes of travel in the 1840s.
(Courtesy of Peter Hall)

passengers and goods, including coal, jostled for steaming room on the same line.

G.N.R. architecture was distinctively solid yet unpretentious, and a nearby example of what it must have looked like still exists at Sandy, seven miles south. There were two platforms, with no waiting accommodation, and linked by a footbridge. On the town side, roughly where the 'Down' slow line is today, could be found the stationmaster's house, ticket office and the platform. The 'Up' platform was not directly opposite this, as today, but began at the bottom of the bridge steps and stretched south towards Cambridge Road.

A New Era – the First Decade

Until 1850, bulk trade in and out of St. Neots was difficult and expensive. The River Gt. Ouse was a partial salvation. Barge traffic plied the river down to King's Lynn with the help of water-level control weirs known as staunches. The barges served two major industries which were attracted to the 'port area', for want of a better term, behind the south side of the magnificent Market Square.

These industries were the 250-strong workforce Bower's iron foundry, maker of wood-burning and gas stoves, gasworks, pipes and steam traction engines serving markets as far away as Australia and Argentina. Nearby Paine's Brewery took advantage of bulk delivery facilities for grain shipments. The Little Paxton village riverside paper mill was also ideally placed to use the river. All barge traffic headed for King's Lynn where ocean-going sailing ships opened up exotic trade horizons.

All this metamorphosed rapidly with the arrival of the railway. Life was changing rapidly for the ordinary traders and peasants of the town now the railway had opened in early August in an atmosphere of anticipatory effervescence. Gone were the days when people felt isolated.

An example of this isolation was the pre-railway age case of a St. Neots woman who had been summoned to Cambridge to receive seventeen sovereigns from a distant deceased relative's will. She had to walk the eighteen miles to the city to collect her windfall but only her head arrived back in town! She hid the coins in her mop of hair before starting home. Half way, at Eltisley, she met a familiar horse-rider who asked her what she was doing, so far from her usual haunts. Forgetting to be discreet, she told the gentleman the full story.

The rider attacked the woman, beheaded her, and stashed her 'hairy ball' in his saddle-bag. He rode off to St. Neots to the High Street's New Inn where he was landlord – and a butcher! In the meantime, another traveller came across the headless corpse and followed the bloody tracks to the inn where the traveller, the town's constable who lived next door to the inn, discovered his wife's head.

By the end of the first month after opening, the G.N.R. announced that it was delighted with the response of the townsfolk to the coming of the railway. The constant rattling of coaches, buses and carts with passengers and goods gave the appearance of a bustling town. Trade had far exceeded the expectations of the company.

After the opening, the station experienced the influx of an enormous range of goods, dead or alive, to arrive at the sidings. On Wednesday October 2nd the first coal agent, Christopher Hall, had begun to import a wide range of coal qualities from well-known seams emanating from a variety of northern coalfields. These included the 'Hard Seam' (Derbyshire), Silkstone (Barnsley, South Yorkshire) and the "best in Western Europe" coking coal Wallsend (a coalmining company in the Auckland Coalfield, Co. Durham). The fire grates of homes could treat themselves at last to this, now cheaper, fuel.

Coal wagons would be sorted at the Peterborough Westwood marshalling yard then delivered daily to stations along the line. Mr. Hall charged two shillings (a florin or 10p) to cart orders to any part of the town to those who could afford between 16-20 shillings (80p-£1) a ton with the Wallsend being top price. If people could not afford delivery they would send their offspring to collect a smaller amount.

Life was cheap; children scurried around the coal-yard, like Third World spoil heap scavengers, leading to incidents when moving wagons or greasy handholds contributed to health and safety issues so readily fobbed off by the word "accidental" dripping off the tongues of coroners and policemen at subsequent inquiries.

The G.N.R. began to learn by its mistakes – the hard way. In 1855, the company offered such a fantastic deal on coal, so people bought in huge stocks of the 'black stuff'. When the offer ended, local coal traffic dried up. In addition, and, at the same time, the company signed an agreement with a London merchant for supplying the Capital from the northern coalfields. When this agreement ran out, in 1857, the merchant concluded a better deal with the London & North Western and Midland companies. The perpetual rumble of coal trucks through St. Neots dried up.

The Times newspaper arrived fromLondon every morning now and was on sale in St. Neots Market Square soon after the arrival of the first train at 9.20am. Another exotic appearance at the goods yard was Lancashire & Yorkshire Abattoir guano, presumably the contents of cows, sheep and pigs' intestines from slaughterhouses. It was readily available at £6 a ton in 1.5 hundredweight (76 kg) bags and was used as fertilizer on local farms. Peruvian guano (seabird droppings) competed for the same market.

If you know any Polish people you may ask them how Polish poultry compare with British species. This sudden easing of communications resulted in these Eastern European chickens being imported and sold on the town's High Street. The daunting task of human emigration also was made so much easier. A "selecting agent" set up business in the town and was interviewing agricultural labourers, mechanics, blacksmiths, bricklayers, carpenters, masons, sawyers, wheelwrights and gardeners at the Priory for permanent homes in Australasia.

Outlying districts were not slow in taking advantage of the new station. Kimbolton, where Catherine of Aragon was banished to

Fig 22 – Station Hotel, St. Neots Station circa 1900 (also known as the Railway Inn). The two goods yard horses stand outside their stable, c.1900. (Courtesy of St. Neots Museum)

its castle, lay nine miles to the west of the station. George Cradock built a horse-drawn Mail Omnibus to rock its way once a day to meet morning trains. The omnibus departed Kimbolton Post Office at 9.30am to arrive at the station in time for the 10.50am Parliamentary train for London, a journey that only took only a shade over one and a half hours. George only had to wait a further fifteen minutes for the arrival of the 11.05am 'stopper' from the London before returning to Kimbolton for half past noon.

Mr. Cartwright, landlord of the adjacent Railway Inn (Station Hotel) at St. Neots Station, took advantage of this potentially lucrative trade by advertising his "excellent waiting room, serving refreshments at the lowest prices". This establishment was sited where the current small car park is to be found at the turn off from Station Road today. It was classed as a hotel by the Great Northern Railway, one of only six listed company-owned hotels in the early Twentieth Century.

The others included King's Cross, Doncaster, Peterborough, Leeds and Bradford so why was St. Neots singled out for such a select building? One can only put it down to the proximity of two eminent local influences. The first was the Duke of Manchester at Kimbolton, who entertained royalty, dukes and lords with their wives. Second, Colonel Duncombe (family of 'Feversham') became a founder director of the Great Northern Railway.

He entertained eminent people also, one of whom was Charles Dickens. He loved rail travel and was invited to Waresley Hall. It was while he was there that he wandered into the village alehouse whose landlady, allegedly, was a certain "Miss Haversham".

It is rumoured that she was the template for one of his characters in "Great Expectations". An alternative scenario, and a more likely explanation, is based on the fact that authors, when looking for inspiration for naming characters in their books, will use friends' names with the odd letter or syllable change. The Duncombe family name is "Feversham"!

Octavius Duncombe died on December 3rd 1879. In just over two months, at the sixty-seventh half-yearly G.N.R. meeting, shadows were cast over the decline of the company's dividend (caused by the contemporary economic depression) and by the disappearance of the Colonel from the scene. At the meeting, he was described by the new chairman, Lord Colville of Culross, as having "the highest character; as conscientious, straightforward, and honourable man as ever lived".

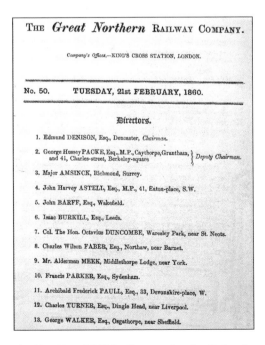

THE *Great Northern* RAILWAY COMPANY.

Company's Offices,—KING'S CROSS STATION, LONDON.

No. 50.   TUESDAY, 21st FEBRUARY, 1860.

Directors.

1. Edmund DENISON, Esq., Doncaster, *Chairman.*
2. George Hussey PACKE, Esq., M.P., Caythorpe, Grantham, and 41, Charles-street, Berkeley-square } *Deputy Chairman.*
3. Major AMSINCK, Richmond, Surrey.
4. John Harvey ASTELL, Esq., M.P., 41, Eaton-place, S.W.
5. John BARFF, Esq., Wakefield.
6. Isaac BURKILL, Esq., Leeds.
7. Col. The Hon. Octavius DUNCOMBE, Waresley Park, near St. Neots.
8. Charles Wilson FABER, Esq., Northaw, near Barnet.
9. Mr. Alderman MEEK, Middlethorpe Lodge, near York.
10. Francis PARKER, Esq., Sydenham.
11. Archibald Frederick PAULL, Esq., 33, Devonshire-place, W.
12. Charles TURNER, Esq., Dingle Head, near Liverpool.
13. George WALKER, Esq., Osgathorpe, near Sheffield.

Fig 23 – List of G.N.R. directors showing Colonel Duncombe in 1860.
(Source – author)

You may know that railway journeys were, compared to today's time-is-money demand for Doctor Who type speeds, somewhat snail-paced. Average speeds in the 1850s were about 40mph for through trains but 'stoppers', serving every station, were down to 25mph. This didn't escape the notice of certain entrepreneurs like Mr. Topham, a St. Neots High Street bookseller. He knew that it took close on three hours to reach London and trundling northwards towards Newcastle was still a lengthy expedition. Travellers' conversations would soon dry up and tedious Tony Hancock-sized boredom would soon grip people's grey matter. So, entrepreneurial Mr Topham stocked what he called "The Railway Library", a huge range of sixty novels featuring topical authors such as Jane Austen and Alexander Dumas. Mr. Topham realised that sex, insanity and violent death would attract buyers, and topics ranged from affairs of the heart to swashbuckling spy thrillers.

What was passenger travel like in the 1840s, even before the G.N.R. came to St. Neots? An insight into this was portrayed by Samuel Watts in 1899, then a recently retired stationmaster at Godmanchester. He said he had worked on the railways for 58 years and began work under George Hudson (1841) when 3rd class passengers could only travel once a day in each direction in trucks without roofs or seats. Railway porters wore top hats, rather like their contemporary cricketers. They were sworn in before magistrates as constables and carried truncheons and handcuffs as well as luggage. The guard had a supply of rockets in case of emergency. The unfortunate postal clerk, who accompanied the mail, had a seat outside the carriage, in the open air, where every possible facility was provided for him

to tumble off and make material for the coroner!

Railway passenger travel began in 1825 but the use of tickets did not start until over ten years later. By the 1850s, ticket fraud had reared its ugly head and inspectors had been introduced. Those of a devious and felonious character floated to the surface and cooked up all sorts of schemes.

On July 19th 1855, Edwin Dibben was collecting tickets from the passengers alighting from the 7.25pm London train at St. Neots. This job resulted in Edwin attending St. Neots Petty Sessions seven days later, presided over by a bench of G. Rowley, R. Reynolds, J. Duberly and S. Newton, all notable local men of considerable 'clout'. In evidence, Edwin stated that he saw the accused, James Howell, approach him from a carriage and offer him a ticket which was from Sandy, a mere seven miles to the south. But the ticket had the date of March 14th stamped on it so the sharp-eyed Edwin told Howell that was not valid.

Howell then apologised saying he had offered the wrong ticket and promptly found another. This was a King's Cross to Hornsey specimen! Edwin suspected a fraud and requested Howell to go with him to Mr. Sparkes, clerk in charge of the station at that time of day. He summoned the police, presumably by telegraph. When they arrived at the station they immediately turned out Howell's pockets. They were astounded to discover nearly £15 in cash, documents "calculated to excite suspicions as to his character", and nine railway tickets of various dates for different railways, all for short distances. The court ruled that Howell be fined the maximum £2 with £1.9s costs. Mr. Williams, the G.N.R.'s inspector, said he had come across many cases of ticket fraud but this was probably the worst in the company's history to date.

Whenever a public company starts to trade there is always the potential for some avaricious self-seeking evildoer who will attempt to beat the system in order to satisfy their desires.

Railway companies were no exception. Already, ticket dodgers were around by 1855, as testified earlier by Howell's court case. The meticulous auditing of financial dealings, from share ownership to the odd penny cash changing hands, were 'booked' and cross–checked by an army of clerks each of whom had to be proficient in the English language and basic arithmetic. There were two classic cases of share dealing irregularities in 1856, neither of them directly involving St. Neots Station.

The more serious one, in a certain December 15th Bankruptcy Court case, targeted the G.N.R. A fairly wealthy and successful share registrar, Leopold Redpath of Chester Terrace, Regent's Park, London, must have been greedy beyond basic common sense because he switched ownership of G.N.R. shares by forging signatures and changing amounts in a most convoluted maze to the tune of tens of thousands of pounds. He was after the dividends!

As a share registrar, Redpath had agreed not to deal in shares after his appointment to the post (Stock Exchange rules at the time). He cleared pure profit of £7,000 in one transaction alone. The final upshot, to keep this story brief, was that it took the jury only five minutes to find Redpath guilty. The judge had the last laugh by confiscating Redpath's property and sentenced him to transportation for life, presumably to Australia. So, if there are any Redpaths in that country they may not wish to know about this tale.

The upshot of this Redpath court case resulted in the next (delayed to March 12th) G.N.R. shareholders' meeting being the most important to date. Many of these people relied heavily on dividends for subsistence but the seriousness and size of the fraud meant that the Attorney-General could not pay any dividend on the 'A' or old share stock of the G.N.R. without the special sanction of Parliament.

The eyes of the country's railway investors were glued upon this case which blew up so soon after the enormously damaging 'railway king' George Hudson affair of 1849. Payment was eventually made after Parliament was satisfied a thorough analysis of all the G.N.R.'s share certificates had been conducted.

Rules Entice Staff to Uphold Company Bye-laws

The year of 2008 has seen the ban on nicotine-fuelled smoky atmospheres in public enclosed spaces come into operation. There is a saying; "what goes round, comes round" and history is full of anecdotal precedents. The G.N.R. had already introduced into their bye-laws a smoking ban on the company's trains at least as early as 1856. Engine smoke was enough!

November 26th 1856 turned out to be a most inconvenient and expensive experience for Robert Lovett, a potato salesman from Eynesbury, a suburb of St. Neots. He was returning from London after a day's business when he was relaxing in a compartment puffing on his favourite pipe with tamped tobacco. Mr. Lovett was spotted smoking at Bishop's Hatfield and the train was stopped at Arlesey Station (or 'Three

Counties Asylum' as it was more aptly named then) where he obediently followed the instructions of the stationmaster.

Before the train left, Mr. Lovett was seen using a 'lucifer' (match) to enshroud himself in smoke once more. The stationmaster returned to the fray whereupon the accused became insolent, made quite a jest of it and refused, claiming that others in the carriage were indulging. Why should he be singled out?

Mr. Lovett was summoned to appear before St. Albans Petty Sessions on a Saturday, about a fortnight later. Mr. Williams, the G.N.R. superintendent, represented the company. He said that company policy was that, if people extinguished their tobacco upon the first request, that was the end of the matter and no further action was taken.

The Chairman of the Bench asked why this case had been brought up at St. Albans. Mr. Williams said that it was customary to take a case to the nearest court to where the offence occurred. Hatfield could not be used because this type of offence required two magistrates but only one attended Hatfield Court. After the evidence had been read out Mr. Lovett pleaded guilty immediately. While sentencing, the distance from St. Neots was taken into account by the Chairman who, in mitigation, reduced the maximum fine from forty shillings (£2) to thirty (£1.50) with expenses of £1 2s 0d.

The reason for pushing for the full fine soon became obvious when Mr. Williams said it was customary in such cases to award half the penalty to the witness! The Chairman questioned this but then agreed that 15 shillings should be awarded to the Arlesey stationmaster. Mr. Lovett dutifully paid in full on the spot, and all of it was handed over to Mr. Williams. That was how petty crime was dealt with in those days.

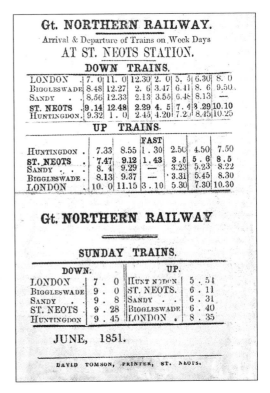

Fig 24 – 1851 G.N.R passenger timetable for local services.

(Source – St. Neots Chronicle)

A Great Day Out in London

Back in August 1840, the Midland Counties Railway started the idea of excursions for the day, at half the price of scheduled fares, to specific attractions. Thomas Cook, of Melbourne near Derby, was the first private individual ever to organise such a trip which was from Leicester to Loughborough.

The G.N.R. was not slow in taking up the idea for 'days out' either in London or at the delightful sea air of Skegness at the end of the only G.N.R.-accessible coastal location. Potential trippers were implored to buy their tickets at least two days before the great day so the company could plan demand for carriages.

In 1855, an enormous attraction was the

magnetic internationally famous Crystal Palace, moved to Sydenham in south-east London after the Hyde Park Great Exhibition of 1851. The G.N.R. dangled the idea to the masses with an announcement that, not only would they be able to visit London, they would also be able to buy tickets at St. Neots Station for London Bridge Station (owned by a different company) and entry to the greatest 'greenhouse' ever built. The idea of buying 'through tickets', to the south side of the capital, had been in existence as early as the mid-Nineteenth Century. Fares to King's Cross were a hefty six shillings (30p) for a first class ticket while the working class could pay half this price for a wooden seat – for two and a half hours! Neither class was resplendent with toilets so one had to plan one's fluid intake before the journey.

One specific excursion was planned for August 20th 1855, a national holiday. The train was due to begin at Tallington, a village four miles due east of Stamford and a most unusual starting point, with first class and covered carriages. There would be no infamous open-top farm animal wagons. They had been banned by the 1844 Act of Parliament which had decreed that passengers must have, in all three classes of travel, a roof to protect the fare payers from inclement weather. First class carriages had soft seats and glass panes in the windows whereas the second and third class covered carriages had minimal open sides, no glass and unpadded seats.

Passengers' clothing in these primitive carriages was frequently soaked, covered in soot or occasionally set alight by flying cinders. The range of Victorian expletives must have plumbed the depths of contemporary language when the train passed through the Hitchin and Copenhagen

Tunnels on the way to King's Cross.

Come the day and crowds of clean, well-dressed working people were seen wending their way up the Cambridge Road towards the station. Excitement and laughter increased in volume. These good folk had walked for miles from villages around St. Neots in anticipation of a mouth-drooling experience. They might even see Queen Victoria, such was their lack of perspective in understanding the sheer size of the Capital.

Innumerable vehicles and horses jammed Station Road and, at 7.42am, the due time of departure, there were nearly five hundred chattering, bubbly and happy-go-lucky ticket-holders standing like a noisy penguin colony on the London-bound platform (there were only two lines and platforms until 1898).

This scene lasted for one and a half hours before the train finally steamed into view! It had been delayed by similar thronged melees at Tallington, Peterborough, Holme, Huntingdon and Offord leaving a mere ten seats up for grabs at St. Neots. You can imagine the indignation voiced at the station staff and defensive guard trying to get a word in edgeways. Panicky and strenuous telegraphing ensued to Peterborough.

The G.N.R. should have known very well what the demand for seats was because of early purchasing of tickets, but no decisions were taken to guillotine further sales or arrange a duplicate train.

An engine and a 'means of conveyance' were found. The train eventually rolled up at St. Neots nearly an hour later, only to throw oil on a raging fire of discontent. This really was the last straw. What upset the potential passengers was the mode of transport being offered by the company for, behind the

Fig 25 – The cattle truck (centre), alternative excursion 'carriage', 1841.
(Source – History of the Midland Counties Railway Co.)

engine was a rake of bullock trucks, open to the elements, no seats and sides of planks with wide draughty gaps!

The people were invited to enter but the vast majority aggressively declined. Profanity and ironic humour began to rule the hour. The few who did climb aboard, as a last resort, rapidly vacated them in deference to the bovine noises emanating from the throats of the adjacent platform masses.

Enter yet another ingredient into the mixing bowl of discontent. A scheduled train, heading for King's Cross, arrived. It was virtually devoid of passengers so the crowd invaded the carriages en masse despite resistance from the company's servants. Once the latter realised their protestations were futile they demanded the difference between the excursion and ordinary fares.

Within a few minutes, yet another special train arrived, hot-foot from the Huntingdon direction and took up many of the passengers. The station was taking on the ambience of a shunting yard! By this time, a considerable number had asked for their money back and gone home. Those who did make the trip arrived in London three-and-a-quarter hours later than the advertised time. Heads must have rolled in the G.N.R. as an inquiry was promised to those who officially lodged strong letters of complaint.

Undaunted by this tale of woe, the G.N.R. ran a similar jaunt, to London, in the following July after an 'in-house' inquiry. Despite the previous year's chaos the company sold tickets through the G.N.R's coal agent Christopher Hall's office in Cambridge Road. Tickets were available right up to the time of departure. Children had free tickets if they were under three, and half price if they were under twelve, that being the school-leaving age at the time.

Scepticism for this trip's success potential ran rife amongst the townsfolk but 230 of them plucked up courage and turned up at the station by 7 o'clock anticipating a train to arrive from Peterborough. The G.N.R., stung painfully by their previous experience, greeted the faithful with their very own train hissing in a siding.

Mr. Sparkes, the stationmaster, and his staff could not have been more helpful if they had tried. The day was eventually so successful the company decided to run more excursions, and they were hoping for six to eight hundred to be attracted to the trips then in the planning stages.

Going on to 1866, local excursions by train were neither limited to the St. Neots Station route nor to such chaos of the type that occurred way back in August 1855. On February 26th, 1866 the Midland Railway opened a line from Kettering to Huntingdon via Kimbolton. That company also seems to have learned the lessons of quality organisation the hard way.

Kimboltonian masses were invited to buy tickets for a day excursion to Hunstanton seaside resort in north-west Norfolk. Over a hundred persons waited eagerly on the isolated station's platform, over two miles from the town, for the seven o'clock 'special' to arrive. The train finally arrived "full to overflowing"; only one or two scrambled aboard. The disgruntled mob was told that a duplicate train was following which duly arrived – but was more jam-packed than the first! Even the brake-van was full of sweaty pleasure-hunting humanity.

The Midland Railway decided to allow the trippers to catch the next scheduled train, at 9.30am, which terminated at Cambridge. A further connection at King's Lynn found the hot and tired travellers arrive at Hunstanton at 2pm with only five hours, instead of the promised nine, to indulge in the sandy delights. Today, you would expect a resort to be pre-warned if a large horde was to descend upon the town at such a late lunchtime hour. This did not happen; with appetites sharpened by the journey in the first two trains, in conditions resembling the Black Hole of Calcutta, the relieved trippers rushed to the hotel seeking sustenance on a broiling day only to be told that they had stopped serving lunch. And people complain today that it is no joy going out for the day in the car only to be stuck in some hour-long motorway tailback as if this type of episode had never happened before.

Other excursions in the 1850s, from St. Neots Station, were limited to the G.N.R. network and by the length of time it took to travel to destinations that were attractive enough to fill a train. In 1847 a temperance movement, called the Band of Hope, was founded in Leeds in the midst of an alcoholic epidemic. Maybe there should be one today!

A Band of Hope promotional meeting was held in Boston, Lincolnshire but the day was 'sold' to the St. Neots' public as an opportunity to visit and climb the famous Boston Stump, the magnificent 82 metres-high church tower, the tallest non-cathedral church tower in the world and attend the famous 'rag market'. The actual travel arrangements were excellent but the two hundred promenaders from St. Neots were not amused by the lack of local supervision in Boston.

Thousands, including a number of St. Neots' females, attempted to ascend the staircase of the famous Stump but were prevented due to their rough handling and coarse treatment by "abandoned vagabonds" who hoped to glimpse a bare ankle or two. The mind boggles!

The popularity of excursions was confirmed by the 1862 analysis of these cheap day tickets issued at St. Neots Station. The excursion season lasted only from June 1st to October 28th and the final tally was 2,454 with Tuesday July 29th being the busiest with 250 merry souls jumping aboard. The season's first was the least popular with only 36 tickets sold.

A later excursion destination which rapidly grew in popularity was the journey to Skegness. This was founded at the end of a branch line, opened just in time for the 1873 summer, and took advantage of the first stretch of golden sand after the uninviting marshes of The Wash with its clouds of mosquitoes, and locals still suffering the vagaries of the ague, otherwise known as malaria.

The 1874 excursion arrived at 'Skeggy' about 11am, just in time to eat lunch that consisted of a meat dish for 3.5p and a glass of beer for 0.5p (or a cup of tea for 2.5p – little wonder alcoholism was rife). People wandered onto the beach and went paddling with naked feet while St. Neots Station employees played a cricket match against Skegness Station staff. Children were being encouraged by nursemaids to write the alphabet in the sand and make moulds of animals with wooden spades, all in preparation for a science and art examination at South Kensington.

The more enterprising men hired a crewed boat and set out for Hunstanton across The Wash. They had to abort the trip after a short time, however, because the intrepid sailors soon fell seasick in the choppy sea. Others used the mobile bathing cabins so as to sea bathe in discreet comfort for fear of showing any naked flesh. There were four miles of beach with donkey rides for 2.5p, and men with guns trying to shoot seagulls for sport at Gibraltar Point. It was mused that this might be a good place to build a hotel!

The G.N.R., in its promotion of an excursion, tended to link an attractive destination with a specific event at that locality. Any excuse would do. I'm not sure how many Irish people lived in the St. Neots area in March 1876 but the G.N.R. ran a trip to Alexandra Palace where a national celebration of St. Patrick's Day was to be held.

By this time, the G.N.R. had direct running rights access to Nottingham, along the grandly-named "Ambergate, Nottingham, Boston & Eastern Junction Railway" branch, from its 1850-opened mainline at Grantham (new Peterborough to Doncaster section). So folks, how about a day out in Nottingham to sample the delights of the famed Goose Fair, the Autumn Races and attend the Industrial Exhibition Day?

Excursions developed into a good business

Fig 26 – A typical gathering at St. Neots Station eagerly waiting for an excursion train circa 1930s. (Source – Joe Doncaster Collection)

for the railway company as local employers started to entertain their employees and their families with outings, usually to the seaside. The firm would discuss the requirements for private saloons with the stationmaster; on some occasions there would be enough bodies to hire a whole train for themselves.

Oh, how the excitement built up during the day. If there were any town band members they would play their instruments on the way up to the station. The platform noise would make townsfolk realise that the isolated peripheral location of the station wasn't such a bad idea after all. George Bower's Iron Foundry supplied 150 jolly folk on a Saturday in October 1885 on the London excursion.

July 1889 saw a ground-breaking development when the St. Neots Wesleyan Methodists showed what could be achieved with sensible negotiation and common-sense when they organised a Skegness day-trip for their Sunday School party of 160 all travelling at the concessionary 1s 6d rate (7.5p) up to two years above the usual twelve age limit. A year later, all the Wesleyan town churches clubbed together and booked a complete train. The platform was chock-a-block with 800 promenaders heading for Skegness once more.

If an individual party wished to book a saloon it could be easily accommodated by a chat with the ever-happy stationmaster. Farmer Preedy, of Caldecote Farm, Abbotsley (3 miles distant) took 46 of his farm labourers and family members to, yes, you've guessed it, Skegness, all in one saloon coach. Jordan & Addington, a large food-processing employer in the town, reserved two saloons on an adventure to Grimsby and Cleethorpes. If a company did not book ahead they took pot luck and had to run the risk of last minute cancellation and 'attitudes' on the factory floor.

There have been some flamboyant sights at St. Neots Station over the years. In February 1898 a 20-strong scarlet-clad party of Cambridge University undergraduates, whips to hand, paid for a special train to bring them to St. Neots to hunt with the Oakley Hounds. I suspect George Wilkinson, grandson of Octavius and contemporary Cambridge graduate, had a hand in this jaunt.

The flexibility of what a stationmaster was officially able to get up to was shown when, in July 1901, none other than Lady Rothschild unexpectedly arrived at the station. She was being driven in her car to Newmarket when the tyres punctured near the railway bridge. Her Ladyship simply abandoned her car to the chauffeur, walked to the station, ordered a private engine and saloon, and travelled the rest of the way in the lap of luxury.

Excursions became increasingly popular after the Great War of 1914-18 but charabanc-type buses began to compete for this trade especially when parties were small. The G.N.R. countered this by stopping express trains on their way to London to pick up day-revellers. The largest railway excursions steamed off to Skegness after the G.N.R. had merged with other companies to form the L.N.E.R. (London & North Eastern). In June 1938, with yet another war looming, it took two trains to convey 1,170 excited people to Skegness.

Royalty and the Railway – "Excuse me, Ma'am, can I have my Plate Back?"

Once the excitement of the new railway's opening had settled into the daily pattern of life, Queen Victoria gave the line the royal seal of approval using it to Scotland and other parts of the country. The first of these journeys caused great excitement in St. Neots, and local people flocked to the station to show their loyalty in an unusually wide variety of aspects.

Local prominent businessmen dug deep into their pockets, dusted off a few moths and cobwebs from purses, and paid for over fifty banners to be displayed sporting such slogans as "The Church and Queen", "The Queen God Bless Her", "Prince Albert and Agriculture", and "Old England For Ever". In addition, forty smaller banners were made for the local charity schoolchildren to wave to Her Majesty. As a bonus, the famous Wombwell's Menagerie was visiting the town at the time and its excellent brass band was hired to join the melee on the platform

To cap it all, a general holiday was proclaimed, the commercial hubbub of the High Street evaporated and the church bells rang in celebration. By 3pm the station was decorated with the banners, the charity pupils were arranged at a spot which gave the appearance of being 20th Century trainspotters, and the band was adding an appropriate cacophony of sound. It was claimed that the whole of the town was there in its Sunday-best 'glad-rags' if an estimate of 4,000 expectant onlookers was near the mark.

At 3.20pm a pilot train dashed through the station, ever wary of sabotage even those days, heralding the approach of the Royal Train itself. Likewise, this train headed north in the blink of an eye so that only a few caught a fleeting glimpse of the Queen. The crowd was mortified and trudged in musical procession back to the Market Square where the band played the National Anthem before everyone drifted off home. What did the townsfolk expect? After all, the Queen did not possess such a weak bladder as to require a comfort-break at every station on the way to Scotland.

On subsequent expeditions Queen Victoria did stop at local stations, such as Huntingdon, Biggleswade and Peterborough, but never St. Neots. The only St. Neots' man who appears to have gained an audience with 'Ma'am' in a railway situation was Joseph Barringer, town High Street baker, who was also an expert viticulturist and "maker of fine champagne". He began to cut grapes from his vines in his large Church Street hothouse in July each season, and he was determined to attempt to present a bunch of his best to Her Majesty.

The Queen was due to alight at Peterborough on early September 11th 1858, en route for Leeds, just as Joseph's grapes were ripening. He journeyed to the city station armed with a bunch of his choicest grapes determined to present them on his best silver dish to, apparently, a "most grateful Queen".

Prince Albert, who, allegedly, eventually scoffed the lot, was especially pleased with the visual quality of the grapes offered by Joseph when he was granted permission to approach the Royal couple. The grapes were displayed on Joseph's best silver dish, but he was dismayed to see it and its contents disappear onto the train.

The dish did eventually re-appear at St. Neots Station some days later when it was returned to Joseph via the local stationmaster – minus the grapes.

The Duke of Manchester

Although the Duke of Manchester was, and is, not Royalty, his use of St. Neots

Station was considerable. His instructions, to various agents, occasionally involved the Royal family. The Duke lived in his castle on the edge of Kimbolton, eight miles west north-west of St. Neots, and his town had its own station from February 26th 1866. It was owned by the Derby-based Midland Railway Company and different from the G.N.R.

Relationships between the Duke and the Midland began on a very sound footing, especially as the Duke had made a lot of money from the exaggerated compensation for the compulsory loss of land during the building of the line. Travel was so much more comfortable and faster.

Before 1866, the Duke's usage of the railway was purely through the equidistant Huntingdon and St. Neots stations, opened in August 1850. If he wanted to travel north or to Sandringham, near King's Lynn, he would use the former while travel to London was via the latter. Sandringham was going to turn out to be a popular destination!

The Duke had developed a regular trade through St. Neots Station's goods yard for his wine, beer and spirits. He was so fond of his Madeira wine that he summoned a cellar man, Alex Bellamy, to visit the Castle on December 16th 1856 to classify his Madeira cellar. The Kimbolton horse-omnibus would be at St. Neots Station to meet the King's Cross train.

On various dates during 1863 the Duke's usage of the goods yards at St. Neots was considerable. On June 25th arrangements were sent to a Mr. James Gray, King's Road, Chelsea for the delivery of a greenhouse, to be collected from the Station. Iron girders for the Castle came through the Station at the end of August 1863 but, as they were delivered late, a full refund of £1.16s.9d was agreed with the G.N.R.

Between September 1863 and January 1864, a wide range of the Duke's goods and animals passed through the goods yard. On September 10th a ton of soap was ordered from Lambeth Soap Works in London. An order for one thousand oysters, in two barrels, was sent on the penultimate day of the year, from Mr. Wiseman in Southend, suggesting the Duke may have heard of their possible aphrodisiac qualities!

The Duke was well known for his horses and he sent some to Compiegne, via the Station, to northern France so that he could go riding there five days later. This activity was confirmed after accommodation on the Dover to Calais boats came through.

A more complicated transaction was completed at the same time when the Duke bought six merino sheep from Habrough, near Grimsby, with orders for them to be forwarded by rail. It was obvious to the goods agent that the Duke of Manchester lived in Manchester; of course he did! The sheep were duly delivered to Manchester's rail stockyard incurring extra cost to the Duke to have them re-routed back through Sheffield to St. Neots.

During the course of the first three days of March 1864 the Duke's agent was instructed to contact Monsieur Laffitte in Paris, who was acting on behalf of the buyer, le Marquis de Galliffet, prominent army general in colonial wars, civil unrest and the Crimean War. The Duke had sold a horse, for £50, to the Marquis, who was recovering from serious wounds during battle. The horse was to be transported via Folkestone and Boulogne after enquiries had been conducted regarding costs and expenses. Once the cheque had arrived on March 3rd the horse was sent to St. Neots

Station after Mr. Hill had bought new clothing and knee caps – for the horse not le Marquis!

From December 27th 1876 to February 19th 1877 the Duke had a series of arguments with the Midland based around the fact that the latter would not provide him with passenger trains when he wanted them! He decided to transfer much of his considerable trade to the G.N.R. St. Neots Station instead.

The first episode involved Queen Victoria's son Edward and his wife, Prince and Princess of Wales, who missed their connection at St. Ives for Wisbech and San-dringham because Mr. Spriggs, Kimbolton stationmaster, failed to telegraph forward to hold trains for the Royal couple; he had to travel via Cambridge. The couple returned a fortnight later to Godmanchester Sta-tion and a guard of honour mounted by the Duke's 'Huntingdonshire Light Horse Regiment'. The Prince and Princess visited the Duke often, via St. Neots Station, an 1870 example of which will be discussed later in the book.

The Duke's argument with the Midland Railway seems to have built up over a period of time since the opening of the Kettering to Huntingdon Railway, culminating in an incident, on February 19th 1877, when a telegram was sent to James Allport at the Midland Railway's Derby central office asking for a modification to the local train timetable.

The following event appears to have been started the evening before when the Duke held a ball at the Castle in honour of his guests. He also invited along a certain Mr. Peppercorn from St. Neots!

The Duke and friends were to travel to London by the 9.15am train but they would have to return on the G.N.R. via St. Neots because the Midland route via St. Pancras to Kettering train would leave the party 'kicking their heels' at Kettering Station for far too long before the departure of the 7.35pm train to Kimbolton. The Duke thought it would be a good idea to ask the Midland to re-schedule the train to an earlier time so that the party would be "in time for an early dinner" and allow the revellers to hunt with the Pytchley Hounds (2 miles south of Kettering). The Midland declined the request thus causing a polarisation of attitude from the Duke. Relations soured thereafter.

There were many further examples of the Duke of Manchester's usage of St. Neots Station over the next few decades but those recounted above give you an excellent idea of the range of activities and incidents involving the Duke and St. Neots Station.

The Importance of the Barnet Railway Act of 1864

In 1864 the G.N.R. was granted an Act of Parliament to build a branch line to Barnet in the leafy suburbs of north London. Why should the reader be bothered with this, you might ask? Clause 12 of the Act added the far-reaching consequences of allowing the G.N.R. to acquire the right to form direct links and running rights with the Metropolitan, South London Junction and London, Chatham & Dover Railway Companies.

This convoluted plan allowed the G.N.R., and St. Neots' excursionists, direct access to the Crystal Palace via the adjacent Sydenham Station. Additional benefits gave the G.N.R. access to a passenger service to Victoria Station from where northern passengers

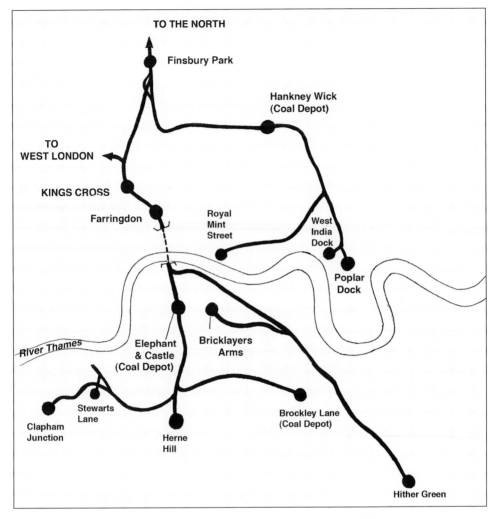

Fig 27 – G.N.R. routes and coal depots in South London south of the Snow Hill Tunnel under R. Thames. (Drawn by Paul & Jenny Todd)

could embark for all points south to the coast and the English Channel ports (using the associated companies' transport).

The G.N.R. then developed South London coal depots, via the 1866 Farringdon (or Snow Hill) Tunnel, adjacent to King's Cross. The rapidly-burgeoning volume of coal, the origins of which were described earlier, resulted in between forty to fifty London-bound trains being dispatched daily from Peterborough New England marshalling

yards and steaming through St. Neots.

Coupled with a similar return of rattling empty wagons, St. Neots was not a quiet station. The north-south direct link was closed in 1907 to Victoria Station-bound passengers, but goods services lingered until 1962. The tunnel faded into the recesses of the memory, in moth-balls, until the Bedford to Gatwick and Brighton idea ('ThamesLink') began service in 1985.

By 1880, another local travel agent, besides

Thomas Cook, was on the scene organising cheap day excursions to London and Skegness, both on the same day. A further excursion was organised, again to London, a week later on September 28th to watch the Australian cricket team play against England at Crystal Palace.

Accidents

Accidents! It is a word that conjures up nightmares in the traveller's mind at any speed in any conveyance. They vary from great inconvenience, with knock-on temporary effects on thousands of other nomads, to utterly life-changing (if survival blesses the sufferer) experiences to both self and family.

In the earliest days of rail travel all sorts of myths were invented surrounding the development of passenger rail transport. The story of the man, with a red flag on horseback in front of an engine to ensure a maximum speed of 12mph, was rife among the local communities; this warned people

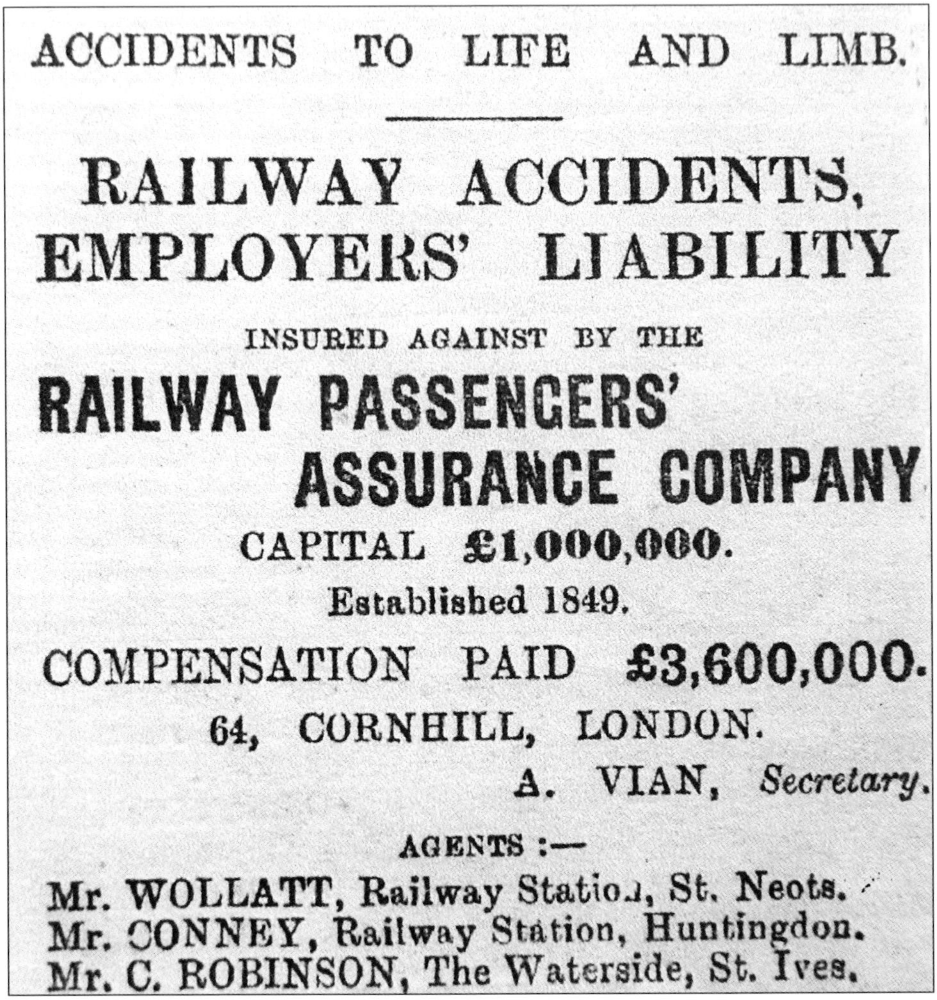

ACCIDENTS TO LIFE AND LIMB.

RAILWAY ACCIDENTS, EMPLOYERS' LIABILITY

INSURED AGAINST BY THE

RAILWAY PASSENGERS' ASSURANCE COMPANY

CAPITAL £1,000,000.

Established 1849.

COMPENSATION PAID £3,600,000.

64, CORNHILL, LONDON.

A. VIAN, *Secretary.*

AGENTS :—

Mr. WOLLATT, Railway Station, St. Neots.
Mr. CONNEY, Railway Station, Huntingdon.
Mr. C. ROBINSON, The Waterside, St. Ives.

Fig 28 – Railway insurance on offer in local newspaper advertisement in 1885.
(Source – St. Neots Chronicle)

that the fiery monster must be avoided at all cost. It was believed that, if a train travelled faster than the fleetest coach and horses of the day, the human body might disintegrate. One wonders how much all of this was generated by vested interests in the road coach trade Experience, however, allayed all fears, and today we can savour bullet and magnetically levitated trains reaching speeds of over 300mph safely.

Accidents occurred on the new railways at all too sickeningly regular intervals. The G.N.R. was no exception, and the first decade of St. Neots station was a particularly difficult and disruptive time for the company and travellers from St. Neots. There have been a surprisingly large number of fatal accidents in the vicinity of St. Neots Station over the lifespan of this nodal point. To write about the details of all would comprise a book on its own if the details of G.N.R. and coroners' reports were included. This led to a selection of such horrendous experiences being described with the bare bones of the remainder that came to light listed at an appropriate section.

Modern rail travellers can be highly vocal, especially in the ruder elements of the English language, when they are informed of late or disrupted journeys due to unfinished engineering work. What happened to the St. Neots' traveller when something went wrong northwards? A classic example of this scenario occurred just three years after the Peterborough-Grantham-Doncaster stretch opened in 1852. Alternative routes at this time were very rare partly through scarcity but also by lack of travel (or 'running' agreements) between the rapidly expanding number of railway companies.

Four miles south of Grantham, the mainline Stoke Tunnel bores its way through

the southern tip of the Lincolnshire Edge, a Jurassic escarpment. Its alternating shales, mudstones and oolitic limestones can be unstable at times and, unless the engineering is of a high standard, is prone to cause disruption. In November, 1855 part of the roof fell in!

Much dangerous engineering work had to be undertaken but, in the meantime, trains had to be kept running, if not to time. There was an alternative route to the North for the G.N.R. The Loop! This kept the company's through-trains running but this second umbilical cord was cut when an accident occurred on the Loop, and that incident resulted in the complete closure of the long-distance schedules of passenger, goods and coal trains for London.

The 'casualty' was a coal train. A dark November Sunday evening, at 9pm, is probably the most inopportune time for a breakdown. Stixwould Station, ten miles south-east of Lincoln on the Loop, was the scene of a coal train rattling south at a good speed with thirty wagons each loaded with seven tons. An axle snapped on one of the leading trucks and momentum compressed the rest into an untidy heap. How the local domestic fire-grates must have roared that winter!

Unfortunately for the company, communications were destroyed by the felling of a telegraph pole with the rupture of the wires when the accident occurred. Boston was eventually alerted but the King's Cross 8.50pm mail train was well on its way. Frenetic activity ensued at the crash site in an attempt to clear a single line, because "the Mail must not be delayed", but to no avail. The Mail Train was delayed for nearly five hours.

Many other accidents, some exceedingly serious, continued to plague and disrupt the

Fig 29 – A breakdown train with steam crane in the 1860s. (Source – 'The Iron Roads')

flow of traffic through St. Neots Station. Occasional incidents at the station caused quite a stir in the first two decades of the line's existence. It must be remembered at this point that, when an accident happened, the injured were not transferred to local cottage hospitals, that is, if they existed, for stitching together. A large number of cases were domiciled in lodgings and local hostelries, often for several months, where local doctors could treat them.

The first local identifiable fatal accident was on Wednesday January 24th 1856, and involved a line repairer (a platelayer) who was walking down the line towards Huntingdon Station. He had been drinking for too much of the day, was hit from behind and killed instantly. The quality of his job was also called into question.

Traffic was affected by another local fatality three weeks later, on February 13th. A gardener by the name of Mr. Daniels was killed by the 5.43pm St. Neots' train for London. He was trespassing on the line towards Sandy when the train overtook him, knocked him down and passed over one of his sprawled arms, separating it entirely from his shoulder. This led to him bleeding to death.

Only nine days elapsed before another local character met his end. On Wednesday February 22nd a parliamentary train was heading towards London at Great Paxton, a mere mile and a half from St. Neots Station, at a "rapid rate". It had just reached the bridge at the farm of Mr. Jabez Paine when

Fig 30 – G.N.R. engine – a typical visitor through St. Neots Station in 1890.
(Source – J. J. Tomlinson's presidential address 1890, Institute of Mechanical Engineers)

the train driver saw an apparently feeble old man attempting to cross the line. Before the driver could warn the man of his danger, or even slacken the train's speed, the engine and carriages, all heavily laden, passed over him.

The accident was observed by several farm labourers in the adjoining field. They rushed to the scene and beheld the gruesome spectacle of a man's body cut in half, the upper part being scattered down the track. The upper torso, or what was left of it, was barely recognisable and armless. Subsequently, the poor man was identified as 94 years old local man Mr. Ashton. The coroner could attach no blame to anyone as the unfortunate deceased was using "the regular crossing", presumably a public footpath.

Axles and wheels were common triggers for incidents. On Friday August 15th 1858, a goods train left Peterborough marshalling yard for London and, when it approached Offord Station, just five miles north of St. Neots, at three o'clock in the morning, the following incident exemplifies how sharp and awake the company's servants had to be at all times.

Smoke was observed, presumably by a signalman, billowing out of a truck containing delicate quality silks and lace from Nottingham. The train was stopped at Offord where the truck was found to be well alight.

Mr. Everard, the Offord stationmaster, organised a gang to clear the line. Subsequent investigations by G.N.R.'s Inspector Williams suggested the fire may have been "spontaneous combustion" after he had visited the Nottingham factories where the lace had been delicately created. The value of the goods lost amounted to £300 (today c. £17,000).

Shoddy Finishing at the St. Neots Iron Foundry? Or at the Station?

In the mid-Nineteenth Century, St. Neots was not renowned for metal-working except for a bell foundry. George Bower, mechanical engineer-cum-innovator extraordinaire, was to change that for a few decades.

George Bower built a tremendous reputation for his gas appliances manufactured at Vulcan Foundry down Fisher's Yard at the rear of the magnificent St. Neots Market Square. At his most expansive he employed close on two hundred and fifty people building gasworks (including for the Viceroy of Egypt and Col. Duncombe at Waresley Park), wood-burners, steam plough and threshing engines. He invented gas stoves, gas meters, patent rust-proof cast iron roof tiles and patent stable floor bricks to save horses damaging legs and hooves. His steam engines varied from three to six-horse power with prices ranging from £40 to £75 in the 1860s.

The company was an important user of the station's goods yard, often lifting heavy products with the yard's crane. Heavier castings were manufactured in his foundry in West Hartlepool in south-east Co. Durham. Gasworks were exported via St. Neots Station especially to towns along the G.N.R.; many of the establishments were in Lincolnshire whose railways were dominated by the company.

It was on Monday September 29th 1862 when Bower anticipated successfully completing a contract to build four steam threshing engines for export to St. Petersburg, Russia via Hull Docks. The engines were pulled up the mile-long Cambridge Road to the station and loaded on to flat trucks ready for adding to the late evening local

PORTABLE STEAM ENGINES.

Fig 31 – George Bower's steam traction engine, 1860. (Courtesy of Linda Reed)

Fig 32 – A steam traction engine, 1858, in the little-changed large St. Neots Market Square awaiting dispatch. Bower also acted as agent for Shuttleworth engines, and it is not known whether this photo is of a Bower or a Shuttleworth type. (Courtesy of Linda Reed)

goods train bound for New England Sidings at Peterborough. With a toot and a chuff the train left, heading northwards towards Offord Station Crossing.

At about one o'clock in the morning, an 'up' London-bound thirty-truck coal train came into collision with something on the line close to Offord Station. The 'object' was so big and heavy it threw the engine off the line, after which it destroyed twenty metres of platform, ran down a shallow embankment and rolled over. The tender, now detached from the engine, also rolled over and finished on the 'Down' line. Trucks were broken and smashed up with coal being strewn all over the area.

Twenty-seven year old Johnson, the engine driver, and Henry Lee, also 27 and the fireman, were both killed. Johnson was killed instantly but Lee 'lingered' for an hour. They were found under a truck, the former horribly mutilated with legs adrift, chest staved in plus other frightful injuries. The stoker had a truck resting on his crushed leg. He begged the guard not to remove him but, as Lee was bleeding and needed urgent treatment, that course of inaction was not an option. He was removed to the Porters' Room in the station where Mr. Everard, still the stationmaster, did his best after sending for Mr. Woolley, the Buckden surgeon who lived a mile distant. Lee died before Mr. Woolley's arrival.

The inquest was held three days later in the nearby Offord 'Swan' public-house and chaired by Mr. Mellor. The details of the deliberations are intriguing and I will indulge your patience while I recount them so that you can see how a verdict of "accidental death" was invariably arrived at after such investigations.

Fig 33 – A suave George Bower in his prime. (Courtesy of Dennis Tinley)

Several witnesses were examined including George Bower and some of his workers. By this time the accident had been cleared and the cause identified. It was a huge circular fly-wheel that had dropped off one of the steam thrashing engines as the truck bearing it clattered over Offord Crossing. The following contains statements made by the various witnesses summoned from as far distant as Grimsby:-

John Bennett – "I am George Bower's foreman. On September 29th, four portable steam engines were conveyed from my master's premises to the G.N.R. St. Neots station to be conveyed to Hull for shipment to St. Petersburg, Russia. The fly-wheel of each machine was keyed in the usual way to the shaft with a single key. Before the engines were taken out of the workshop I tried each of the keys of the fly-wheels, and drove them home. Each wheel was rung at the same time as if all were solid together and I considered them all perfectly safe. I did this in order to satisfy myself about the safety to travel on the railway. I tried every nut and everything that could loosen and found all secure."

James Ayres (a working engineer for G Bower) – "I fitted the fly-wheels to each engine. I am perfectly satisfied all the keys were in the fly-wheels when they left my hands."

Coroner – "Do you think any one of those keys would work out?"

Witness – "I do not think it possible. I think it would be something in the packing. I heard they dropped the engines down in the truck."

Mr Bower – "This sad incident will teach us not to send another engine away without taking the fly-wheel off. I heard of one dropping off a while ago. No engine shall ever leave my premises without the wheel being off. I want it to be understood that I do not wish to implicate the Great Northern Railway in this matter although I do not think the Great Northern has sufficient accommodation for such things at St. Neots, and Mr. Dance would no doubt admit this. It appears to be one of those accidents of which it is impossible to find out the cause but which we know how to prevent in the future.

I know my foreman is a very careful man – he never lets a piece of work go out scamped, and if there was the slightest blame to us I should never forgive myself for such a sad accident."

George Shawley, foreman station porter, St. Neots Station – In the loading of the engines they did not sustain any damage but they all were dropped about two to three inches (6cm) in the same way on the truck. I do not think they sustained any injury by being so dropped. Sleepers were spiked before and behind the wheels on each truck and ropes were attached to the truck buffers from the wheels of the portable engines to make them secure while travelling. The engines were covered with tarpaulins and partly boxed – that is, cased with woodwork. I did not observe any of the fly-wheels loose nor anything defective about them."

Charles Edward Hopwood – I am agent to the Great Northern at Grimsby. On Wednesday morning last I saw four portable steam engines at the Great Northern's docks At Hull. They were for shipment to Russia. Engine No. 1 was without a wheel but the wheel had been sent separately. Engine No. 2 was without a wheel. No. 3 was also without a wheel, and No. 4 was quite complete, the fly-wheel being keyed on."

A Juror – "Where was the No. 3 wheel?"

Coroner – "It was found at Corby Glen (south of Grantham)."

Mr. Townsend Dance – I live at Peterborough and am one of the district superintendents of the Great Northern. On Tuesday morning last I saw on the railway, near to Offord Station, a fly-wheel of a portable steam engine. It was marked 'No. 2' and broken in three pieces."

The Coroner then summed up and the jury returned a verdict of "Accidental Death" in both cases. Also, they recommended that fly-wheels should be removed, for security of persons, to prevent similar accidents.

At the inquest's closure, Mr. Bower liberally expressed himself in commiseration to the widows, as willing to give ten pounds towards their relief. This triggered the Buckden vicar, Rev. E. B. Turner, into opening a fund on behalf of the two widows and children which raised a further £8 15s (£8.75p).

St. Neots Station goods yard was not immune to fatalities. Shortly before twelve o'clock on the morning of December 9th 1879, nineteen year-old Charles Pedley, a steady and well-behaved young man who was generally respected by colleagues, was shunting some trucks (with the help of a horse as was common for 100 years) when he became trapped between two of them. Charles had been working on the railway for only four months when he was conducting this unsupervised manoeuvre.

One of the trucks moved unexpectedly when Charles' back was turned. He was centrally placed, which was unacceptable practice, when the silent move occurred. His body became the target of the coupling hook on each truck.

Foreman porter William Cook witnessed the accident and ran to help Charles. William picked up the unfortunate victim who uttered one or two incoherent words before breathing his last (this incident occurred in today's main station car park area).

The inquest was held at the Station Hotel, on the very next day under the deputy coroner C. B. Margetts. The jury listened to the evidence, as portrayed above, and spent little time before returning a verdict of "accidentally killed" with no suggestions of further enquiries to look into health and safety practices like today. The last two incidents, and the subsequent decisions at their coroners' courts, would have caused tabloid headlines of protest in today's 'climate' of health and safety.

Statistics of Railways in 1856

In 1856, the local St. Neots Chronicle reported to the local people that the famous railway surveyor and engineer Robert Stephenson MP, son of George, had submitted to Parliament a table of national railway facts extolling the enormity of the industry's size after just thirty years of existence. Members of the House were not paid by the State until 1911 so, in those days, their finances came from personal estates or from lobbyists who were willing to cross the palm with silver to entice someone to push forward their plans.

Here is what Stephenson said:-

More rails are laid down than are enough to form a belt of single iron round the World.

The extent of completed railways now (1856) in Gt. Britain and Ireland is 8,054 miles.

The total cost of these lines is £286,000,000 to date.

There are more than 50 miles of tunnel.

There are 11 miles of viaduct in the neighbourhood of London.

The earthworks of the railways measure 550,000,000 cubic yards.

The excavated earth would form a pyramid a mile and a half high, with a base larger than

St. James Park in London.

Eighty million miles are run in the course of a year by the trains.

There are 5,000 engines and 150,000 working vehicles.

The engines in a line would stretch from London to Chatham, the vehicles from London to Aberdeen.

The various companies employ 90,000 officers and servants.

The engines consume 2,000,000 tons of coal annually.

In every minute of time, 4 tons of coal convert into steam 20 tons of water.

In 1854, 111,000,000 passengers were conveyed on railways, each journey averaging eleven miles.

1854 railway receipts amounted to £20,215,000 which is nearly half the amount of the ordinary revenue of the State.

Every railway company's receipts have continued to increase.

20,000 tons of iron require to be replaced annually, on account of 'wear and tear'.

26,000,000 wooden sleepers require to be replaced annually.

300,000 trees are felled annually to make good the decay of sleepers (creosote was not invented until 1858).

Trains carry an average of 200 passengers.

The cost of running a train is under 1s. 3d. (6p) per mile.

500 passengers at 0.625 of a penny (0.3p) per mile, produces 5s.2.5d. (26p) per mile.

But for the facilities offered by the railways, the penny postage scheme could not have been carried out.

£70,000,000 have been paid to landowners and others as compensation for property interfered with by the lines.

The Electric Telegraph extends over 7,200 miles requiring 36,000 miles of wires.

3,000 persons are employed by the electric telegraph.

40,000 men are employed indirectly.

1 in 50 of the entire population of the kingdom is dependent upon the railways.

The saving of a farthing (0.1p) a mile in the expense of running the trains, would make a difference of £80,000 a year to the railway companies.

Success in Reducing the Accident Rate

As you have read, accidents were extremely common on these early railways and, in 1874, no less than a shocking 1,425 people were killed and 5,050 injured. Travellers were urged to buy cover for a journey from the Accidental Insurance Company's agent in St. Neots' Market Square which was offering £1,000 upon the death of an unfortunate railway accident victim.

At the 1875 Bristol inaugural address of the British Association (founded 1831), the incoming president Sir John Hawkshaw concentrated on contemporary "Railway Travelling" in his address to the annual meeting.

Sir John spoke at length about railway safety and compared the United States much-improved safety record with that of the United Kingdom. He said that the U.S. railways, with their unfenced tracks inland, were prone to wild animals such as buffalo straying onto the tracks. That is why they added huge searchlight-like lamps to the engine fronts. They also developed the continuous brake system linking an immediate co-ordinated response from all the carriages together by means of an air brake system controlled by the driver.

Two experiments were carried out

at the end of July 1874 on the London Underground Metropolitan Railway. The first used a self-acting method of extracting foul air from the tunnels by a pneumatic tube. The other was the use of the continuous vacuum brake imported from the U.S.A. Both were successful.

There was a move to introduce this brake system in the U.K. but was resisted initially by the railway companies because of cost. They used the excuse that British tracks were protected by secure fencing throughout so should be able to see imminent danger and act appropriately. They also 'swept under the carpet' the fact that engine crews were prone to drink-driving. Sir John countered these arguments by saying that British engines had no headlights, and a driver's only response in an emergency in the daytime was to shut off the steam, apply the engine's brake and quickly jump off the footplate! The fireman had to be awake and alert at all times to ensure he wasn't left behind.

A positive national campaign to reduce this carnage on British railways, led within a year to the setting up of a trial to highlight the effectiveness of the continuous brake system being promoted at the time.

The National Railway Commission, in conjunction with the Railway Association, invited continuous brake systems' competitors into joining in a trial of the various methods then in existence. Next time you travel by rail, you may cogitate about this little tale.

The trial was held on the Midland Railway lines, about two miles west of Newark over a distance of four miles towards Nottingham. The Parliamentary observers were the Duke of Buckingham and the Earl of Aberdeen. Four systems were represented along with splendid spanking new engines and carriages from five different companies and all conforming to the same length and weight.

In front was the London & North Western train with the chain brake of Clarke & Webb. Next was the Caledonian with the automatic reaction brake followed by the London, Brighton & South Coast with its Westinghouse vacuum brake. The Great Northern came next with James 'Vacuum' Smith's vacuum brake, and then four trains from the Midland sporting various systems.

The trials were so impressive the Board of Trade made continuous braking systems mandatory. Because of the expense involved the various companies introduced the most reliable over the next few years. In 1881, the G.N.R. chose the continuous vacuum brake system which automatically applied the brakes if the pipe split open for whatever reason – a fail-safe method. This, then, is the story of how your train journey was made safer after the intolerable pre-1870s carnage.

Shady Dealings

A G.N.R. employee at St. Neots Station, one Charles Waddell, aged 23, was brought before St. Neots Petty Sessions on December 12th 1878 for embezzling G.N.R. money on three counts while employed for the past four years as a clerk at the station, latterly as the chief clerk in the goods office.

Mr. Richard Williams, now a Superintendent in the company's railway police force, said he came to St. Neots on December 6th to formally interview the defendant in the Railway Tavern and to tell him that he, Waddell, was to be prosecuted by the G.N.R. directors for the mighty sum of £52 2s 4d belonging to the company. In addition, he would be charged with falsifying the company's accounts. The prisoner said he intended to repay the money when his brother gave him some cash, as if that would let him off the hook in those Dickensian times. Waddell was then arrested in the Station Hotel, taken to the police station, and placed before the magistrates the following day and remanded.

The whole affair had come to light when St. Neots' citizen Alfred Jordan (founder of today's Biggleswade-based cereal bar and muesli industry) visited the station to take receipt of goods and pay for delivery at the same time. The cash was not entered in the "Receipts Book". A simple total statement of the day's takings, without a detailed break-down, was then handed to Mr. Heslop, clerk-in-charge at that time of day. For once, the latter decided to put the books under closer scrutiny. He sensed something nasty might be lurking in the goods shed considering the size of Mr. Jordan's order along with 22 other customers that day for only £4 7s 10d!

Waddell was further charged with embezzling £2 14s 4d over Mr. R Smith's trade as a soot merchant. These were black days for Waddell indeed. Charles Morris, the G.N.R.'s travelling auditor, then went through the station's accounts with a fine tooth comb and found over £50 missing. The hearing was adjourned and, very surprisingly for those days, the prisoner was allowed £100 bail and two sureties of £50 each.

The Travelling Post Office

The Travelling Post Office, or TPO to 'anoraks', was a remarkable system that helped deliver next-day envelopes all over the U.K. It was a railway service, with special sorting carriages, linked to the Royal Mail. You could even post letters into the carriage at the departure station if it was for a destination along the route.

The first mail carried by train in the U.K. was as early as 1830. The first mail sorted in a moving train was in 1838 in a converted horse box. So successful was this speedy service that the last road mail coach working out of London was withdrawn in 1846, tying in with the bankruptcy of the Cock Inn, Eaton Socon. The service through St. Neots was introduced in the early 1850s after a battle with Rowland Hill, the Postmaster-General penny-black stamp instigator, who preferred the Rugby route to the North.

These mail trains ran every night along most main lines. They deposited their mail bags en route and snatched incoming ones without a hint of slackening speed. This was done by means of a specialised gibbet known as 'the apparatus', supporting a net strong enough to resist a Bobby Charlton net-buster of a shot. Another apparatus would hold bags to await the snatch and up to eight could be dealt with in one fell swoop.

There was one drawback to this system. The engine crew sometimes had to poke out their heads to see where they were (there were no satellite-navigation systems or radios around in those days). Occasionally, they got the timing wrong.

This story relates to July 16th 1874. Josiah Wiles was born in 1810 in a house in St. Neots High Street to boot and shoemaker William (where Moore's Walk/Barclays Bank are sited). Josiah duly followed in dad's boots, so to speak. He took on a number of service trades one of which was being 'lured'

Fig 34 – Travelling Post Office line-side apparatus. (Source – Brian White)

into the brewery trade as the landlord of the Peacock Inn situated close by the Engine & Tender Inn. The Peacock still exists but as a derelict whitewashed shell 100 metres town-side of the railway bridge. Josiah also took in boarders to supplement his revenue.

In 1874, St. Neots Post Office was sited next to the main entrance to Paine's Brewery on the south side of the Market Square (relocated in 1913 to its New Street site). The collection of the mail bags was sub-contracted to an agent, and Josiah offered to do the job. It would be a nice little earner for him, trotting up to the apparatus on the south side of the Cambridge Road railway bridge with his pony and trap, pick up any bags from the nets on both sides of the tracks and set the relevant bags, collected earlier from the post office to be snatched and whisked to their appropriate destination. The apparatus could deal with the delivery and receipt of two bags each in a single drop and, after the following incident, a "fix on" notice system was installed just to the north of Potton Road Bridge. This system was a white illuminated rectangular board located

line-side which could be seen even during the depths of a dark foggy night.

On the fateful evening of July 16th 1874, Josiah went to do his duty and found that the expected bags had been delivered but the bag due to be 'snatched' aboard the train was torn asunder with its contents scattered along the track towards the station. As Josiah left the apparatus to go back to the town post office, he clambered down the embankment and made his way to the road adjacent to the bridge where he saw the body, who turned out to be 25year-old Alfred Bugby (engine fireman and Peterborough resident), lying on the north side of the bridge parapet with his brains lying on a shoulder. The station sent some assistance to the scene and removed the body to the station's south goods shed.

In those days inquests were held in the nearest decent-sized room, usually an inn. In this case the Station Hotel was chosen as the venue. The apparatus is sited a mere 45cms (18 inches) from a passing engine and it was assumed that the fireman, whose body it was, had leant out of the cab to fix

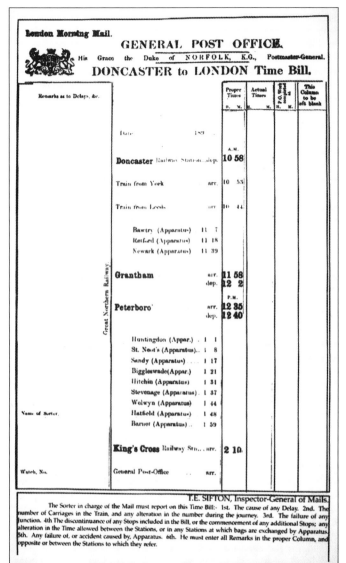

Fig 35 – Doncaster to King's Cross nightly TPO timetable schedule serving St. Neots, 1897. (Courtesy of Nene Valley Railway)

his location at a most unfortunate moment.

The TPO train was the 9.15pm from King's Cross and, as it was a heavy load on this occasion, was being pulled by two engines. Alfred Bugby was fireman in the second engine. His driver, James Simmons, did not notice Bugby's disappearance until a while later. He whistled the first engine to stop but the crews could not find poor Alfred so continued to Huntingdon where Simmons alighted and returned to St. Neots in a light engine to see what had happened.

Joseph Wiles stated that, in his opinion, the pick-up apparatus was far too near the track. The Coroner's jury, holding court at the Station Hotel once more, agreed, and shortly after, the G.N.R. moved the apparatus further back. The jury returned another "accidental death" verdict.

It is extremely rare, possibly unique, for such an incident to occur a second time in the same spot on the railways. St. Neots is different! Almost fifty years to the month later, on Wednesday June 14th 1925, a copycat style of head bashing on the TPO apparatus at 2.25am on an express goods and TPO train saw Fireman Mercer hit his head on the post holding the catching basket as he leant out of the cab. This action he did periodically to see that his exhaust was not wasting water.

The driver sped on to Tempsford where Mercer was transferred unconscious to the 'guard way' (the guard's compartment as it was known). Meanwhile, the stationmaster telephoned to Hitchin for a doctor and an ambulance to meet the train for rapid transfer to town's hospital. Fireman Mercer died at 7 o'clock the same morning. At the inquest the G.N.R. said that this type of incident was rare, and it had only occurred once before, at Hitchin in 1889. You now know this was a bit of a tall story.

Mercer's driver on that fateful run was a relatively new cab mate because his previous driver, Mr. Denby, had been killed when he fell out of the cab at Hitchin Station on February 14th, four months earlier, into the path of another train which chopped off both legs leading to him losing consciousness as his life blood drained away. Carnage reigned supreme at times on the railways for another body was found on the tracks, this time between Tempsford and St. Neots later the same day, after someone had fallen from an express train. There must have been a massive disruption to the flow of traffic along the whole line.

A third TPO fatal accident occurred, this time a mile north of Sandy Station, on Tuesday evening June 1st, 1937 and involved a driver for the L. & N.E.R. The details are not within the remit of this book. Let it suffice to state that the driver's head was in collision with the apparatus and caused severe damage yet again to the brain's function.

Short Change for Sunday Duty on Railways

On the evening of Monday September 1st 1875 the "Belmont Tavern", on York Road, King's Cross, was the place to be if you were employed by the G.N.R. Traffic Department. A sardine-packed meeting of a fledgling union, entitled the 'Amalgamated Society of Railway Servants' (the very first railway union), was being held to discuss the one-sided terms of employment of guards and signalmen in the Traffic Department of the Great Northern Railway.

The employees' gripes emanated from the insistence that railway companies generally were expecting their guards and signalmen to work seven days a week, where Sunday trains ran, for only six days' pay despite the fact that the drivers and firemen were paid for the seventh day. Is it surprising there were rumbles of discontent? A unanimous resolution was passed to the effect that the Sunday shift be limited to ten hours for guards, eight for signalmen and six days constituted a week's work.

Railway Passenger Duty – An Unfair Tax

The earliest railways were built to improve coal transport. The 1829 Clarence Railway, near Stockton on Tees, did not introduce passenger services until six years after opening and at about the time when the Stockton & Darlington owners had become exasperated with the growing corruption amongst the drivers (who collected, and kept, some of the fares). Tickets were invented at about this time to reduce this revenue leakage.

The Government of the day, ever keen to seize on an opportunity to increase its own revenue, introduced a tax on ticket receipts. It became known as the Railway Passenger Duty. The railway companies tried every trick in the book to minimize the effects of this by introducing such schemes as 'excursion fares', or selling a third of the tickets and issuing the rest free to lucky travellers. This only exacerbated the problem; they ended the year paying up to 28 per cent tax on gross receipts. This system was altered by an Act of 1842 to a flat rate of just 5 per cent upon gross receipts.

By 1870, suburban commuter traffic patterns were already well established. Workmen's trains were common, encouraged by an Act that required certain trains to stop at every station and charge no more than one (old) penny per mile. There would be no tax on these tickets.

There was great pressure to abolish this tax, especially from the big suburban companies. The Government, however, did not want to lose out and did not want the companies to profit from distances of, say three quarters of a mile and still charging a penny. The main argument was that these city companies felt they were being unfairly penalised when other railway companies, whose bulk of revenue from coal, iron ore and dock traffic, were getting away scot-free of tax. In March 1875 a large deputation from the House of Lords visited the Chancellor of the Exchequer to ask for a repeal of the Railway Passenger Duty.

Another deputation followed, this time from the London Trades' Council demanding the removal of the tax on fares below one penny for some of London's railway companies were ceasing to run workmen's trains. In true politician's style Sir Stafford Northcote (later Earl of Iddesleigh) said he promised to give the matter his best attention. Of course he would!

By August of that year no action had been taken and the repeal or, at least an amendment campaign began to increase its pressure. Railway companies provided the Exchequer

Fig 36 – Tempsford and St. Neots tickets & luggage labels from 1904 to 1950.
(Peter Hall & author's collections)

with £700,000 a year in revenue and that was absolutely essential if the Government was going to continue to balance its books (remember at this time income tax was minimal which benefited those with large incomes). Had the Government got in its sights the forthcoming Afghanistan War of 1880-5 that cost £950,000? That had to be budgeted.

Campaigners for changes to the Duty were demanding that, if repeal was not in the offing, at least the Government could more fairly deal with this 'carbuncle' by taxing the net profits of the companies. This would offer justice to all. People all over the country were engrossed in the battle of wits not least those in St. Neots. The Government, however, weathered the storm of protest for another 54 years. No changes were made to the tax until 1920 when the minimum fare, of a penny per mile for third class workmen's tickets, was raised to 1.75 pence per mile. Finally, Railway Passenger Duty on all fares ceased to plague the railway companies in the Finance Act of 1929 at the same time as the eruption of the Great Depression hit people's jobs and the world's economy.

Return Ticket from St. Neots to Moscow by Train Only – What a Prospect!

This was not really a pipe dream. Articles began to appear in the St. Neots press in the mid-1870s about a tunnel under the English Channel to connect with the French railways.

A consortium of British and French rail companies had resurrected the 1857 idea of a tunnel in 1874. By early 1875 the two governments were negotiating goods tariffs and were succeeding in reducing 'international difficulties'; it had become as detailed as that. In 1876 French geologists surveyed the Channel's rocks using divers holding their breath! The stable chalk bed, that ran from Shakespeare Cliff, Folkestone to Sangatte, Calais, was chosen, and Sir James Brunlees was appointed engineer in charge of the project. He had built docks, viaducts, Southend Pier and railways around the world (including the Huntingdon, Buckden, Kimbolton & Kettering Railway) and was an internationally- renowned engineer.

The French and British began boring simultaneously in 1881 using an 1875-patented rock boring machine run on compressed air. Progress was rapid, and the workers were transported to the chalk-face by shuttle wagons again using compressed air. Eventually, trains would be run on the same traction, to eliminate smoke and steam, until electricity could take over.

A few months after construction began, French and British politicians began to quarrel big time over the ownership of the Suez Canal and African colonies. By 1883, British military generals had become so nervous they pulled the plug on further progress even though the scheme had already excavated two tunnels, each two kilometres long, at both ends. The British company offered to fund a permanent guard, in charge of a dynamite booby-trap, for use if the French mounted a surprise attack.

The dreams of St. Neots businessmen, such as George Bower, bit the dust. Later, in 1914, First World War generals pined for the tunnel, ironically claiming that such a link would have shortened the conflict by two years.

The idea was resurrected in 1973 when the United Kingdom joined the European Union but the Wilson government ran into serious financial difficulties in 1977 and the scheme was mothballed. The Thatcher government gave it a third chance, and with North Sea oil and privatization money swelling the coffers, set about digging in 1987 with a 1997 grand opening. Now you can catch a train from St. Neots to Moscow – or even Vladivostok! An old friend has recently travelled by train from a Lincolnshire village station to Rome.

Another Glimpse of Royalty

Although Queen Victoria never graced the platform at St. Neots the station has had its moments. The nearby Kimbolton Castle, a magnificent Tudor architectural monument and the banishment home for Catherine of Aragon after Henry V111 'flung' her to one side, sits in what was in 1870 superb hunting and shooting country. It was also the seat of the Duke of Manchester whose ancestor was linked with Oliver Cromwell. The castle is now a fine and successful private school.

In March 1870, the Prince and Princess of Wales arrived at St. Neots Station en route for Kimbolton Castle. This time, the station's decorations were not wasted including those around the temporary portico erected in the front of the booking office. The 'Special' train arrived just after 6 p.m., disgorging its celebrity passengers from the saloon carriage. They then ambled to the station entrance on a carpeted way along either side of which were double ranks of the 1st Huntingdonshire Rifle Volunteers and the County Militia Band. From there they left for Kimbolton through the town in a four-horse open carriage and cheered all the way by admiring crowds. A week later, the reverse trip was played out; same Rifles,

Band, carpet and cheering crowds where the special train was waiting to whisk the happy couple back to London.

At the beginning of December 1879, one cold Saturday morning, a train stopped at St. Neots Station and disgorged two resplendent young men from a specially provided saloon carriage. They were met by a small contingent of the cavalry of the Duke of Manchester's Volunteer Regiment (forerunner of the Civil Defence) which escorted them through the town in style.

Who were these two men? They were the wonderfully named Prince Ferdinand of Schleswig-Holstein-Sonderberg-Glucksburg and Prince Louis of Battenberg. They were not only cousins to one another but also to Queen Victoria. The former was a member of the royal family of Prussian Germany, still feeling pride from the defeat of France in 1870. The second prince was the father of Lord Louis Mountbatten and grandfather of the Duke of Edinburgh. Prince Louis became the First Sea Lord for two years from 1912 but was forced out of office due to his German roots when the First World War blasted its way on to the scene. They were visiting George Victor Drogo Montagu (aka Viscount Mandeville) soon-to-be the 8th Duke of Manchester, for a session of fox hunting.

The two princes left after a few days in the same carriage attached to the 5.49pm Huntingdon train en route for Sandringham for a short visit to the Prince of Wales. Two days later the Duke and Duchess of Manchester also left for Sandringham by the 12.37pm train, presumably after a little shunting and transference of these special passengers through Huntingdon's second station at the time to access the Fen route via Ely to King's Lynn. This type of special

Fig 37 – Prince Louis of Battenberg (Mountbatten), grandfather of the Duke of Edinburgh. Visitor to St. Neots and Kimbolton Castle in 1869.

(Source – Internet)

passenger to-ing and fro-ing must have been a fairly regular 'trade' in those days.

By 1903, security along the Royal Train's route had been tightened to such an extent that only twenty people went to the station in May to see Edward VII pass en route for Scotland. For the local police, life was more hassle than pleasure as they had instructions to man every bridge and station, presumably to stop any potential assassins.

Lighting Railway Carriages – St. Neots Shines the Way

Modern rail carriage electric lighting is very efficient, but it wasn't always like that! Flickering candles and rape seed oil lamps were no match for the draughty compartments especially in the early days

when the windows had no glass. A number of entrepreneurs were attempting to make a name, and a fortune, for themselves by attempting to invent gas systems that would last entire lengthy journeys.

It is well known in specialist circles that Julius Pintsch (pronounced "pinch") of Prussia, the main Germanic state before unification in 1871, had developed a compressed oil gas system that had been purchased by Prussian railway companies (1869). It is far less known, if at all, that St. Neots also had its very own gas equipment inventor! One George Bower, no less.

There was nothing Bower wouldn't turn his imaginatively creative mind to, and rail carriage lighting taxed his fertile inventiveness around 1860 to 1870. Living on the main East Coast route, Bower had experience of that dreadful carriage lighting and set about attempting to make life more tolerable and safer on dark evenings and in tunnels.

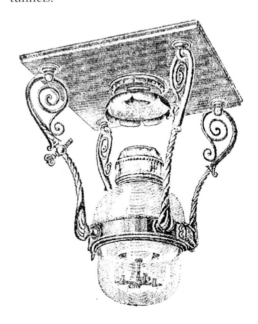

Fig 38 – Pintsch's oil-gas carriage lamp in 1870.
(Courtesy of Dr Mike Sharman)

It is difficult to ascertain as to who was first on the compressed gas cylinder scene, Bower or Pintsch. A bit of a battle developed between the two systems, both trying to produce the brightest most economical light using compressed oil gas (this may have been methane). Pintsch gained further contracts with U.S. railroads in 1881.

Bower, on the other hand, had formed a link with the G.N.R. in 1878 to conduct trials between King's Cross and Edinburgh (even though the G.N.R. only ranged as far north as just beyond Doncaster). The U.K. began to suffer a major economic depression at this time and the G.N.R.'s traffic was feeling the 'pinch'. The company insisted on certain restrictions in the trials that cut costs to the bare bone. They insisted on the cheaper fuel, and coal gas had to be used instead of oil.

This was a real challenge that Bower solved with the greatest success. Although coal gas was less effective he solved the light intensity by enriching (carburetting) the coal gas with naphthaline, again derived from coal.

In the 1860s, Bower's gas was contained in narrow carriage-width torpedo-shaped cylinders but by 1880 the gas was contained in a pipe-shaped 20-centimetre diameter, 5-metre long tube. Both Pintsch and Bower types were compressed to ten atmospheres. The trials showed that this was sufficient to light a four-compartment carriage on a return trip from London to Edinburgh, the tube lasting for ten hours. The cost of lighting a single lamp for the entire journey was one paltry penny (0.4p)!

The problem of full gas cylinder availability was solved by Bower. He built small gasworks at strategic stations for refilling empty ones! His first was at St. Neots followed by further gas ovens at Aberdeen (for the Scottish North Eastern Railway), Essendine (G.N.R. near Stamford), Hellifield (M.R. near Lancaster), Audley End, Low Leyton, Marks Tey (all Eastern Counties Railway), Ellesmere Port (Shropshire Union Railway & Canal Co.), and a number of stations in Spain, Italy, Russia and India. Exports were sent through the docks in London, Liverpool and Hull. This was quite an active and thriving industry with great prospects.

Whatever transpired from all of this, between the three corporate bodies isn't known, but Pintsch's system was being used by the G.N.R. by 1895 as shown by the illustrated cheque issued by the G.N.R. to the "Pintschs Patent Lighting Co.". The cheque was signed by "F. Shuttleworth", a G.N.R. director who is famous today for the Shuttleworth Air Museum, Old Warden,

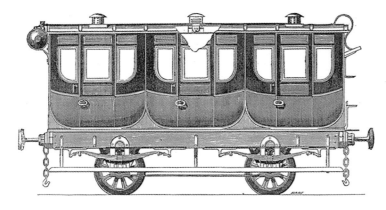

Fig 39 – Bower's gas cylinder and G.N.R. carriage gas lighting system, 1870.
(Courtesy of Linda Reed)

Fig 40 – G.N.R. cheque paying Pintsch & Co. for gas, signed by Col. Shuttleworth, director, of Old Warden, 1895. (Source –author)

Biggleswade which is situated on his old family estate.

George Bower suffered very badly from the non-payment of supplied goods in many parts of the world including a wood-burning stove contract with an Argentinian dealer. It is possible that Pintsch gained the G.N.R contract as a result of this unfortunate tardy South American deal, along with a number of other unpaid contracts, which left the company devoid of development funds. This resulted in Bower's bankruptcy in 1885, and dealt a severe blow to industry in St. Neots.

A Fast Train

St. Neots Station has existed for over one hundred and fifty years and in that time, being on the East Coast Main Line, it has seen many magnificent engines enthrall waiting passengers as they passed its platforms at speed.

One such engine appeared for the first time in 1870. It was of a revolutionary design with a distinctive seven foot (2.1m) diameter driving wheel which was out of proportion to all the rest on the machine. This was the illustrated iconic Stirling single-wheeler designed by Patrick Stirling. On Saturday July 31st 1880, a modified and improved example with an eight foot (2.4m) driving wheel diameter, ran from King's Cross to Scarborough (as the "Scotchman") pulling six coaches which contained a number of dignitaries including the Lord Mayor of London and his retinue. This inaugural run must have received full co-operation from the North Easter Railway Company who owned the 'metals' from just north of Doncaster to York and on to probably the most salubrious seaside resort of the time.

The engine's performance was so impressive the timings and speeds were recorded in meticulous detail. The train departed from King's Cross at 1.50pm, passed through Tempsford in 52 minutes and reached York three hours and 37.5 minutes later after a slow 10mph pass through Peterborough and a ten and a half minutes stop at Grantham. This gave an average speed of 52mph over the full route. Even so, stage timings, such as from Grantham to Newark, reached a dizzy 59mph. The whole journey knocked 17.5 minutes off the usual scheduled run confirming Stirling's faith in his new design.

The Times newspaper correspondent, who accompanied the train, waxed eloquently over the whole experience, took notes on the timings and distances (using the line-side quarter-mile posts and the official Bradshaw Timetable as accurate guides) which enabled him to calculate the average stage speeds between towns along the route.

He was so impressed by the exhilaration created by the journey his description ran away with his imagination to the point that he was convinced the rural moving spectacle, through two and a half degrees of latitude, would have put to shame the trajectory of any brightly coloured meteor that the Times reported frequently! He suggested that, in these troubled Victorian times with massive losses in the Afghan War being reported;"Men who can manage such

Fig 41 – Dinner being served on G.N.R.'s resplendent Pullman restaurant car, with gas lighting, 1885. This was the first service of its kind on British railways.
(Source – 'Railways of Britain' by O. S. Nock)

deeds at home should be able to steer safely and thoroughly through any crisis abroad". I wonder if this could apply to the present day and entrust the running of the country to the best brains in the various railway companies. No, maybe not!

These new engines were extremely popular, and 'corridors' were introduced to allow passengers to walk the length of a train. This, in turn, allowed the G.N.R. to operate their first restaurant car, in 1879, between King's Cross and Leeds. These ornate Pullman coaches on this service had open platforms on each end to help transfer from one coach to another. The decoration throughout the length of the train created such a general air of affluence, the G.N.R. felt they could charge an extra half a crown (12.5p) over and above the cost of their meal! This must have been quite a 'moving' scene as this special train sped through St. Neots Station at 55mph.

Wholesale Dismissal of Railway Employees

A Great Northern Railway Company's announcement, on May 8th 1884, hit the St. Neots Station staff like a bombshell on that day. The national economic depression forced the company's hand to cut costs, and the management made redundant between 1,000 and 1,200 men at a mere 48 hours' notice, 300 being in the London area.

The main workers affected were brick-layers, carpenters, joiners, other artisans and labourers. This suggests a mothballing of all building work immediately. Station clerks faced a ten per cent overall reduction in numbers but no redundancies were announced for the men who operated the trains. Those dismissed did not receive

any benefits, either from the State or the union namely the Amalgamated Society of Railway Servants, and so were thrown onto the labour market at what today would be a totally unacceptable short notice, and at a time when jobs were few and far between. This redundancy situation was repeated by the Great Eastern Railway, with 1,500 dismissals and followed by other companies throughout the land.

Apart from the Depression, a major con-tributory factor involved in this draconian state of affairs for the G.N.R. was the cost of the very high level of damage caused by the collisions in the Canonbury Tun-nel (1881- 4 dead) and at Hornsey Station (1882- three dead), both of which were in the London area.

Who was this Man?

On the evening of the 24th October 1885, at 8.20pm, driver Joseph Rowell released the brakes on his goods engine in New England Marshalling Yards, Peterborough to journey southwards to pick up wagons from station sidings down the line towards St. Neots.

Six stations later, Rowell was on the Cambridge Road railway bridge shunting into St. Neots south sidings at ten o'clock. His engine was adjacent to the TPO apparatus on the south side of the bridge when, in the dimmest light, he noticed three or four objects lying on the tracks. He alighted from his footplate to see what these 'lumps' were. The horrifying discovery at the first 'lump' was that of a human abdomen – no limbs, head or chest.

The other remains were gathered up, including a limb five hundred yards north of the station close to Priory Hill Bridge (aka 'Rowley's Bridge'), by porters and carried to a building at the station. It was assumed the man had been killed by the 'down' train from London but, on enquiring at Peterborough, no evidence of blood or flesh could be seen on any engines, possibly because it had been raining the evening before.

The Coroner's Court, held yet once more at the Station Hotel, could not identify the man. There was nothing in his pockets, and the chance it might have been a missing person from Bedford led to a negative identification by that man's relative. John Rowlett, a local labourer, said he had seen a similarly dressed man hanging about the TPO bridge the previous afternoon who seemed agitated in his movements. The landlord of the "Two Brewers" said he recognised the remains as those of a man he had served the previous day.

The Coroner, Mr. Wade-Gery, summed up by stating that the unknown person was killed on the railway but how or by what means there was no evidence whatsoever. Forensic science today, supported by DNA evidence, would have been much more meticulous in its investigations, but that was the nature of life and death in those days. We will never know.

A New Scheme in the Area?

By 1885, the local railway scene was successfully established. The idea of an east-west railway junction at the south end of the town had long evaporated into oblivion, and was satisfied by two alternative routes. Both radiated from Cambridge with one aiming for Sandy and Bedford while the other headed for Huntingdon, Kimbolton, Thrapston and Kettering. This left great swathes of Huntingdonshire bereft of

railway support. Local pressure groups were springing up around the country, each one desperately attempting to build its own local line to connect with the relevant main artery. Only the odd main route remained to be constructed, like the Great Central Railway from Sheffield to Rugby and London Marylebone.

There was one such smaller scheme, however, right on St. Neots' very own doorstep suddenly hitting the spotlights in 1885. The rural villages between Bedford and Peterborough were more heavily populated in the Nineteenth Century because agricultural mechanisation was only just in its first two decades. These new-fangled steam ploughs, threshing machines and traction engines needed coal and the only way to acquire it at a reasonably competitive price was at a railhead, preferably within a few miles of the farm.

A scheme to fill this railway void, to be known as the Bedford & Peterborough Railway, was conceived and surveyed in that year. Due to local influence it was initially planned to come within five miles of St. Neots, at Great Staughton, but was straightened a few months later to end up near Stoneley and within a mile of Kimbolton. The Duke of Manchester obviously had more 'swaying' power than anyone in Gt. Staughton!

The germinating company tried to drum up support for the idea by holding a public meeting in Kimbolton on Tuesday November 10th 1885 and the following account of the debate was reported in the St. Neots Chronicle. It gives a great insight into how railway schemes were promoted in those days even with their attendant compulsory purchase orders of land and buildings. Compare this with the diverse hassles surrounding today's road and rail plans.

The Proposed Railway between Bedford and Peterborough (Newspaper report from the St Neots Chronicle Saturday November 14th 1885.)

The largest and most representative meeting that has met in Kimbolton for many years assembled in the Girls' Schoolroom on Tuesday evening "to consider the advantages which the Parish may obtain from the above line, and if necessary to petition the promoters on the matter." The vicar, the Rev. Kater Vinter, was voted to the chair, and amongst those present were the Revs. Banham and Ulyett, Captain Duberly, Drs. Hemming and Hellett, Major Hayes and Messrs. Haughton Moulton &c., &c.

The Chairman, in opening, said he was responsible for calling the meeting but he had done so in consequence of a letter he had received from the Parliamentary agents for the line: having conferred with several influential parishioners, it was their unanimous feeling that a meeting should be called to know all about the line. They had representatives of the line with them that night to give the information they required. He would call upon Mr. Butler to give a statement.

Mr. Butler (St. Neots) said: "I became interested in this line at the wish of the promoters and of their Parliamentary Agents. The tract of country between Bedford and Peterborough is now without a railway (not true; the Kimbolton to Huntingdon Railway was opened in Feb. 1866). Anyone who looks at a map of the country will see that a railway between those places is very desirable. If you look at Smith's Railway Map you will be struck by the great gap which lies between the line of the Great Northern Railway and the line of the London & North Western. Through a great part of North Huntingdonshire and beginning from Kimbolton there is no convenient railway accommodation.

"Mr. Raffety, the gentleman who has lately purchased an estate at Great Staughton, is desirous to see this district provided with railway accommodation. He and other gentlemen in London have put themselves to the expense of a preliminary survey. As soon as this was done it was proposed by Messrs. Burchell, the Parliamentary Agents, that I should go along the route over which the railway is proposed, to ascertain whether the people residing on the proposed line cared about it and whether they would assist in obtaining the Bill. Plans &c., have to be deposited by a certain day this month in order to comply with the standing orders of the House of Commons.

"The Bill is next moved into Parliament, and then goes into the Committee Room. All this causes a considerable amount of expense, and the promoters are desirous of asking the people residing along the route whether they are so anxious to have a railway to come forward with funds to help. It is to be hoped that one of the great railway companies will eventually take it up and work it. It fits in best with the Midland system and it is thought they will take it up.

The Midland Railway, however, would not make it in the first instance, as they would have to do all this preliminary work, which would bring them into conflict with other railways. Opposition would thus be invited. But as a landowners' line it escapes that opposition which it would otherwise meet with. Mr. Raffety and I during the last few days have been along a great part of the route.

"One thing there was no doubt about, that the proposed line was everywhere unmistakably welcome. (Hear, hear.) There has not been the slightest qualification about it. We found it rather a slow process, going about seeing one or two people at a time and this is the first opportunity we have had of seeing more than two people together on the subject. We thought it desirable when we got here, the most important point on the line, that a meeting should be called. The original survey was for the line to run farther from Kimbolton and nearer Great Staughton than now proposed.

"The Midland Railway Company will have nothing to say to us until the Bill is obtained, but it was ascertained that any Company would require a line free from curves to run quick trains on, and our original line was not straight enough for that purpose.

"Thereupon those gentlemen who had undertaken the preliminary survey set the surveyors to work again and they straightened the line. The express wish of His Grace the Duke of Manchester was that the line should be brought nearer Kimbolton, and whilst straightening it, it was brought nearer.

"The proposed line now crosses the road on this (Kimbolton) side of Mr. Horsford's house. It then passes up the hill and goes straight to Easton. It passes about a quarter of a mile from Spaldwick and then crosses the next hill about half way between Barham and Woolley.

"Mr. Raffety headed the subscription list with 50 guineas. Mr. Howard of Bedford gave 25, Mr. Welstead (Kimbolton town's gasworks' manager) of Kimbolton 25, and Mr. Murfin, Gt. Staughton 25, and many other people all along the route have subscribed. Any questions those present may desire to ask we will answer, and if you pass a resolution favourable to the line, and let us put your names on the Provisional Subscription List, it will be very valuable assistance.

"The line runs beside the Midland northwards from Bedford until it comes to the place where the branch to Northampton goes off on the left (Clapham Junction). There our line will go to the right. It will curve round Clapham and pass between Keysoe and Little Staughton, nearer to Keysoe than Little Staughton, and thence to Kimbolton."

Capt. Duberly said that the line was projected along a different route to that at first proposed, and would not consequently benefit him half so much. He would, however, make no opposition but do all he could for it (hear, hear).

Mr. Eley (London) said he had had great experiences in railway affairs and felt sure that the line would be a most successful undertaking.

Mr. W J Raffety (Gt. Staughton) said: "Gentlemen, I was going to say, friends and neighbours, I came into this neighbourhood about 12 months ago, and soon found that there was insufficient railway accommodation. I had two excellent men who came from a distance and who would have taken my two farms if there had been a railway anywhere near. I found there was a large quantity of land out of cultivation. I had sundry talks with my neighbour, Capt. Duberly, and several other landowners, and found myself after a time in the presence of His Grace the Duke of Manchester.

"I had previously worked up the feeling of the country and driving from Bedford to Peterborough two or three times I found there had often been talk of a line but nobody had seen their way to start it. Then I had sundry talks with friends in London and found that before approaching great railway companies it was necessary to have a plan of the proposed route and the probable cost. Two or three of us found the necessary funds for a preliminary survey. We now found ourselves close to the time when it is necessary to apply for the Act of Parliament.

"There is a limit to everybody's purse, so to speak, so that those who are going to benefit by it, must now put their shoulders to the wheel and do their part. With this object we have been along the route, and taking the bad times into consideration I am positively astonished at the support we have received. There is not a single individual we have seen but what has subscribed. Up to the present time the big landed proprietors have not been approached in the same manner as the tenants and smaller owners have been.

"I set about to see if it were an investment that large capitalists would be likely to entertain, and I am pleased to tell you that the money for the whole construction of the line has been offered (hear, hear). This is an opportunity that very rarely occurs to any district, and I do think it should be taken advantage of. I hope that tonight all of you who are interested in this will do all you are able to, and I feel sufficient confidence in the large landed proprietors of the district that if a decided expression of opinion is given they will not stand aloof.

"Whilst we benefit a £10 note, they will benefit hundreds and thousands. What interest I have in this part of the country is at Staughton, and I have fought hard for a station there. But we must look at things fairly. The cost will be less if the line is made as now proposed. But even now Staughton will be less than two miles from the station and Kimbolton about one. The Duke of Manchester also very much wished to have the railway nearer to Kimbolton as it would be much better for so many more people. We shall be pleased to answer any questions (hear, hear)."

Capt. Duberly asked how much more money was required for the preliminary expenses.

Mr. Raffety said the total amount was about £5,000. They did not want to make a large profit, or injure any existing company, but simply to provide railway communication for a large tract of country.

Capt. Duberly wanted to know where the £5,000 was to come from. Mr. Raffety said that if all the people down the line would contribute pro rata as those that had already done so, the money would be found half-a-dozen times over.

Dr. Hemming asked if there were any promises from Bedford way. Mr. Raffety replied that Mr. James Howard M.P. had taken great interest in it and said that though it would spoil his Park, he did not mind as it would do a great deal of good.

In answer to Dr. Hemming Mr. Butler said the necessary plans etc., would be lodged before the 30th inst. He did not think the Great Northern Railway Co. could oppose it as it would not touch their line. The line would run into Peterborough on the London & North Western (via the present-day Nene Valley Railway).

Capt. Duberly proposed "that a line between Bedford and Peterborough is desirable." Dr. Hemming, in seconding, said that the line had been wanted for many years. A line from Bedford to Peterborough would greatly increase the value of property in their neighbourhood and they might do all they could to help it. What help they meant to give must be given at once (hear, hear).

The resolution was carried unanimously.

A vote of thanks was then accorded the Chairman.' (Rev. Kater Vinter)"

The scheme did not attract sufficient funding and mortgage offers, and the Bill was abandoned.

Staughton Manor Railway and Romney Marsh

There was one railway to be built in Great Staughton! It was named the "Staughton Manor Railway" and ran east from the Manor for a mile to the village centre. It had one G.N.R. Atlantic-type engine

"Northern Chief", and a Great Western Pacific "Green Goddess", with a 15 inch gauge. The engines were built by Bassett-Lowke of Northampton, still famous to this day as possibly the best model railway engine builders. The owner was millionaire Captain Jack Howey, a Bentley owning Grand Prix racing driver.

His closest friend was Count Zborowski , also a Grand Prix racing driver and owner of the original Chitty Chitty Bang Bang car Bentley car. In 1920, the pair hatched a plan to build a railway, possibly to at least St. Neots. To this end, they attempted to buy the now famous Ravenglass & Eskdale Railway (in the Lake District) but failed. Count Zborowski was killed around 1925 racing in the Italian Grand Prix at Monza leaving Jack Howey alone to realise the railway dream.

Fig 42 – Staughton Manor Railway GNR 'Northern Chief' Atlantic engine at Staughton Manor Station. (Courtesy of Sam Malt)

Fig 43 – Staughton Manor Railway GWR 'Green Goddess' Pacific engine with owner Jack Howey at Staughton Manor Station. (Courtesy of Sam Malt)

Fig 44 – Staughton Manor Railway Bridge over the River Kym at Gt. Staughton.
(Courtesy of Sam Malt)

Captain Howey eventually found an ideal place at Romney, Kent in 1927. He decided to dismantle his Great Staughton railway and transport rolling stock, track, bridge and himself to Romney. The only railway memorabilia intentionally left behind was the signal-box which ended up as a greenhouse in a local garden. When Jack Howey was made a prisoner-of-war, Bassett-Lowke bought the two engines back into their ownership

This new railway at Romney was developed over the next three decades into what is now the famous narrow gauge Romney, Hythe & Dymchurch Railway. The Captain's name is commemorated in Romney by the Howey Hotel and a number of pubs called the 'Howey Inn'. Jack Howey saw all this come to fruition before he died in 1963.

There is no sign of the line in Great Staughton today except for a small amount of track bed near the site of the old River Kym Railway Bridge and remnants of the bridge's parapets after the Home Guard practised destroying such structures in World War Two.

Colliery Suppliers for St. Neots via Paine's Coal Department

A remarkable discovery occurred around the time of the Millennium. Robert Freeman, of Souldrop, Wellingborough visited a car boot sale in Leicestershire and bought a dustbin liner full of late Victorian-early Edwardian paperwork related to the St. Neots Paine's brewery and flourmill. The papers provided an extremely detailed insight into the size and breadth of the company's national and worldwide dealings.

Emerging from this Aladdin's cave of

St. Neots' industrial history was a batch of coal wagon delivery notes, mostly on G.N.R. official printed matter, from several collieries. These origins were concentrated mainly in that Derbyshire-Nottinghamshire border area described earlier. There were also suppliers from the Barnsley area of South Yorkshire and the world-important South Wales Coalfield. Anthracite coal, the most efficient boiler steam-raising and heating variety of the 'black stuff', was bought by Paine's, showing their financial strength at the time. The following table is a sample list of collieries with dates:-

Babbington Colliery, Nottingham	1892
Fforchaman, Cwmaman, Aberdare S. Wale	1903
Shirebrook, N. Notts.	1903
Kirkby nr. Mansfield (owner Butterley Co.)	1903
Annesley Colliery Co. nr. S. Mansfield	1903
Blackwell Colliery Co. nr. Alfreton	1903
Clay Cross nr. Chesterfield	1903
St John's Colliery, Normanton, S Yorks.	1903
Strafford Collieries Ltd., Barnsley, S Yorks.	1903
Wombwell, Barnsley	1903
Birchwood Colliery, Somercotes, E Derbys.	1903
Shipley Colliery (Heanor GNR branch), E Derbys.	1903
Pinxton (Silverhill Colliery) GNR, West Notts.	1903
Cwmteg Anthracite Colliery, S Wales	1903
Duffryn Anthracite Colliery, S. Wales	1903
New Monckton Colliery, Royston, Barnsley	1906
Newland Colliery, St. John's, Normanton, S.Yorks.	1903
Carran Colliery (via P'boro), S Wales	1901
Mountain Ash Colliery, S. Wales	1903
Brynamman Anthracite Coll'y, Carmarthen, S.Wales	1903
Manvers Colliery, Notts.	1904

These collieries supplied between them a mixture of top-quality anthracite from South-west Wales, presumably heading for the company's factory boilers, and quality bituminous coal from the East

Derbyshire, West Notts and South Yorkshire areas probably being sold to domestic households.

Inflation was a problem a hundred years ago but it was not as dramatic as in the second half of the Twentieth Century. The price of coal is a reasonably keen guide to the percentage rate when one compares the tonnage price of Durham 1855 Wallsend black 'nuggets', at 20 shillings (£1) with the 1912 price of the same coal at 25 shillings (£1.25). South Yorkshire Wombwell House 1912 coal was one shilling less, while Nottinghamshire's Mansfield Annesley 'Best Hards' retailed at a mere 22 shillings (£1.20 a ton). These figures give an average annual inflation rate of less than half of one per cent over a 57-year period (1855-1912).

It is worth commenting, at this point, that the Station's goods yards in 1886 were thronged with building materials being delivered to merchants in the town. One such merchant, Daintree & Jewson, was receiving planks, deals, battens, flooring boards, poles, laths, staves, slates, lime, whiting, grindstones, sanitary pipes, Staffordshire goods, fire bricks and flagstones. The 'Jewson' gentleman was the son of the founder of the present-day national company, and this branch was sold to Charles Tebbutt (1887 World speed skating champion) in 1888. He continued the builders' merchant's operation in business until he died in 1944, and the firm survived until the 1990s.

The Aussies Delight in the Taste of St. Neots Beer

There is a saying that "beer does not travel well" but James Paine's Brewery proved otherwise. Based in St. Neots Market Square, the company operated three major subsidiary

Fig 45 – Paine's Beer advert rightfully boasting of its quality in Australia.
(Source – St. Neots Advertiser)

businesses in the town, and they all relied totally on the railway station goods yard.

The first business was the supply of local industrial and domestic coal. Second, the company milled wheat and barley, and produced malt extract for businesses all over the United Kingdom and the world. Third, the brewery fermented barley to create a fine beer marketed as "John Bull Pale Ale". They were so proud of it they shipped it out for a minimum of three years (1879-81) to Sydney, Melbourne and Adelaide, Australia where it won at least two Gold Medals beating the local brews despite being on board ship for 8 weeks! Either the Australian beer was so bad at the time or Paine's beer was a superb traveller even though it had suffered tropical heat on the voyages.

Disaster – St. Neots Station's Greatest Accident

The scene was King's Cross Station just after eleven o'clock on the eve of Monday 15th November 1895. The Special Scotch Express (renamed the "Flying Scotsman" in 1924), as it was called in those days, was standing hissing impatiently and waiting for its passengers bound for the North. The train's crew had arrived and settled in, and were also waiting for their passengers; only twenty seven at the start of the night's journey.

The driver, a proud Grantham man at the top of his trade, was looking forward to this journey, a service introduced in 1862 to Edinburgh with extensions to Glasgow, Perth and Aberdeen by 1895. It had taken a lot of negotiating with three or four other railway companies. The driver was only steaming, non-stop, as far as his home town for 1.26am when another crew would take over. The night was mild and clear of fog so there were no hidden dangers.

The train was composed of two sleeping cars, a Pullman coach named "Iona", four corridor coaches and two brake vans. Pulling this rake was a gleaming apple green engine that was the pride of the G.N.R., a Doncaster-built, now Grantham-based

Fig 46 – King's Cross by night, 1905 – typical scene at the start of a journey north. (Source – author)

Stirling Single, no. "1006", sporting its pair of, now, eight foot (8ft 1.5ins) diameter driving wheels weighing a mighty 19.2 tons. What was not taken into consideration was the increase in piston cylinder diameter, to improve performance, which made up the adhesive weight of the main axle to over 20 tons. Just four days earlier Patrick Stirling, the designer of this engine, had died.

The journey was snooker table smooth at speeds varying between fifty and sixty miles an hour. That is, until St. Neots was reached. The train sped through the station at precisely 12.30am dead on time but, 35 metres before the end of the platform, the sixth carriage became derailed to the left pulling those behind it with it and breaking the continuous brake-pipe. The rails and sleepers were ripped up and the platform edging slabs were torn asunder.

Adding to the potential for disaster was an adjacent line of coal trucks snaking away from the main line under assault. The derailed carriages were now nearer to these trucks and the inevitable collision happened in a split second. Unlike today, carriage construction in those days, although aesthetically pleasing, was not helpful in the preservation of life during such an incident.

The first derailed carriage was totally wrecked, its roof finishing up on top of some of the coal trucks. Its chassis remained as a destructive weapon to the following sleeping car. Its momentum caused its front half also to be demolished, and the same damage was repeated on the third derailed carriage. The brake van was not severely affected and was removed from the scene before the following photograph was taken.

The front half of the train, consisting of the second brake van, Pullman car "Iona" and three other carriages, applied its continuous braking system automatically

Fig 47 – 'Scotchman Express' crash scene opposite St. Neots North Signal box, 1895. (Source – author)

Fig 48 – A further view of the crash scene, 1895. (Source – author)

but still managed a 'fingers crossed' 519 yards (470 metres). It travelled as far as Priory Hill (Rowley's) Bridge before screeching to a halt. These un-derailed carriages had been damaged due to the derailment causing them to rock against the last coal trucks.

Two people not involved with the train jumped into action. The signalman, James Cullip, aged about 27 and Tempsford-born, alerted others up and down the line, set signals at 'danger', gave the alarm to the fogman's house and sent two fitters, who were at the box to clean the signal rods, for assistance. They alerted Mr. Furnace, Station Hotel landlord, who in turn drove his horse and buggy furiously to the town to inform the police. Superintendent Copping and PCs Gale, Wilson and Mortlock hot-footed it to the station, and Dr. Cross of 20 Market Square and surgeon to the G.N.R., arrived half an hour after the accident occurred. Other doctors who appeared shortly afterwards were John Turner (The Priory) and Thomas Gray of Brook Street.

Despite a few fires breaking out in the wreckage Dr. Cross waded into the remains of the sleeping car to see what he could find. Only one person died instantly, a Miss Louisa O'Hara of Crouch End. Her sister, Mrs. McGregor, received only a broken ankle and a few scalp cuts and doubtless, a great deal of trauma.

William Corrie, Woking flax merchant en route to Dundee, was found severely wounded, and moved to another undamaged carriage. He was given a shot of whisky, probably the worst act possible. He died two days later at "Sunnyside", a house in Avenue Road three hundred metres nearer the town.

Others injured included Dr. Trotter of Staindrop, Darlington, provision merchant Sidney Carter of Newcastle, William Cavendish Bentinck (grandson of Lord George MP, Leader of the House 1848) of London and Professor Sir James Dewar (chemist at the Royal Veterinary College, Edinburgh). The rear guard was so badly injured he could not give evidence to the Coroner until three weeks later. Notable people who escaped injury were Mr. Penn, MP for Lewisham, William Appleyard of Middlesbrough, T. Ferguson of York and Lady Rosslyn (young wife of the Earl of Rosslyn, a landowner who gambled away the family estates by 1896 at the age of 26) of Dysart House, Fife.

Those passengers who were either uninjured, or only slightly damaged, resumed their journey north early on the same day in the undamaged part of the train. Today, the whole scene would have been impounded for forensic scrutiny. At the time, this crash, involving a broken rail, was alleged to be a unique accident in the country's railway history.

The nearest hospital was ten miles to the north, namely the "Huntingdon County". The injured could not be moved far and were sent to the town's Wrestlers and Cross Keys hotels. Mr. Fox's private house in Avenue Road was the 'oasis' for Mr. Corrie of Woking, Surrey who was travelling to Dundee on textile business. The latter was pushed through a compartment partition and both his knees and three ribs were broken. Mr. Carter had a miraculous escape. Asleep and lying relaxed in bed at the time of the accident he was flung through a window and found himself on top of a coal wagon with a large piece of plate glass embedded in his collar bone area.

A few of these locally treated injured passengers stayed put, under the care of doctors and trained nurses, until they were well enough to risk an onward journey. The object of delving into such detail is to give you a clear idea of exactly what the medical care was like, after a rail crash, in those late Victorian times after such a severe incident in a town with no hospital and rough unmetalled roads connecting towns.

The Board of Trade Inquiry

The Coroner's inquest, to be held in the Magistrates' Room under the chairmanship of C. R. Wade-Gery and thirteen jurors, was adjourned pending the recovery of the injured and the outcome of the Board of Trade inquiry which was held at the station goods office in February 1896.

The cause of the accident was identified immediately. Investigators discovered that, as the accident evolved, the carriages ripped up the rails and twisted them into cooked spaghetti-like shapes. Two rails, however, had fractured and disintegrated into four and nineteen pieces respectively. Why were these rails different from the others? The inquiry concentrated on these.

Startling facts emerged which led to national manufacturing specifications being introduced as a result of the Board of Trade's final edict and, in my mind, should have had an airing in the October 2000 Hatfield rail crash inquiry because the same basic chain of events occurred.

The rails were manufactured by the Railway Steel & Plant Company of Newton Heath, Manchester (but, by 1895, no longer trading) under a definite specification of eighty pounds in weight per yard length. The two were part of an order from the G.N.R. for 500 tons of Bessemer steel rails supplied in 1872-73. These rails were laid in the 'Up' line (to London) in the spring of 1873 but, as they wore thinner over the years, were replaced in 1886. Those graded as 'serviceable' were stacked in the station North goods yard for use when required, presumably either in an emergency on the main line or in the goods yard itself.

Initial weight tests highlighted the fact that they had been worn down to a mere 70 pounds per yard in the rail that fractured into nineteen pieces and 72.3 pounds in the second (with four fractures). The rails were then sent to Pattinson and Stead of Middlesbrough for chemical and detailed microscopic examination using the new geological/metallurgical microscope. They were founded in 1876 and are still performing a quality analytical service today to the metallurgical industry.

The chemical analysis of the rails brought to light wide variations of percentage carbon, silicon, sulphur and phosphorus content along the two lengths of metal, all of which affected the hardness and brittleness. Apparently, some railway companies at the time demanded better quality control for such a vital piece of material but the G.N.R. accepted this batch for whatever reason.

The microscopic examination identified a series of minute flaws. These did not exist at the time of manufacture but were induced by regular wheel pounding over a period of time; they were invisible to the naked eye after they had developed. Their growth was from the top downwards into the rail, similar to mud-crack formation.

How did these rails come to be used in the main line? Somewhere between 1886 and 1895 someone made the decision to use two of the goods yard-stored 1873 'serviceable' rails to replace two of the 1886 rails. The flaws would have gradually developed over time and accelerated by technological changes in the steam engines now being used on the top services like the 'Special Scotch Express' on that fateful night.

The engine, already identified as no. 1006 Stirling Single, was of the modified type of the class, which only left the builder's workshop eight months earlier in the second phase of the Class's evolution. This meant that, with the slight three centimetre increase in driving wheel diameter, its axle weight had increased to a massive 19 tons 4 hundredweight (19.2 tons). After this revelation, the chairman of the inquiry then urged the G.N.R. Company to increase the weight of its standard rail for main lines to at least 90 pounds per yard and to replace all

Fig 49 – The Stirling Single no. 1006 which hauled the 'Scotchman Express' on the fatal night. (Courtesy of Peter Hall)

the old 80 pound rails where much worn. It was fortuitous that the second "Great Race to the North", held earlier that year on August 20th, was not marred by a similar disaster.

Success creates its own problems

This 1895 Scotch Express crash happened as the railway line was approaching its 50th anniversary. The growth in traffic had been phenomenal especially with coal trains often queuing to continue their steaming up to London.

A complete makeover was needed urgently, for the Cambridge Road Bridge had been extensively repaired over a period of a few Sundays in 1889. This example was repeated regularly along the whole length of the line, and the broken rail disaster was like a straw breaking the camel's back.

Engine development, like the Stirling Single-wheelers, the increasing size, weight and frequency of trains of every description signalled the end of the line in its then present state of inadequacy. An ambitious scheme hit the drawing boards during the 1890s supported by successful Acts of Parliament which agreed to the doubling of tracks from two to four. The complexity of the plan was a bit like adding an extra two lanes to a present-day motorway. The 1897 Act specifically targeted the Sandy to Offord section.

By May 1897 the work on the Sandy – St. Neots stretch rang to the happy hammering of the navvies' endeavours, widening embankments and cuttings, rebuilding bridges and the two stations at Tempsford and St. Neots. At terrible cost to life and limb. Such was the carnage, this 12 mile stretch of quadrupling work earned the reputation

Fig 50 – Irish navvies' clay smoking pipes excavated from line-side one mile south of St. Neots Station. (Ken Barringer Collection)

of costing a life or a limb for every mile of track completed.

The labour force of 150 navvies, many of whom were Irish, was often doubled by extra journeymen and local inhabitants at peak times, so some accidents were inevitable. The photograph shows two clay smoking pipes, from the late Ken Barringer's collection, which were discovered in Eynesbury's eastern cutting of the quadrupled route. The Irish harp motif on the bowl was of the type made in Manchester by Irishmen in the second half of the Nineteenth Century, and was probably accidentally left there by a forgetful Irish navvy after a meal break.

The first fatality associated with these excavations on this stretch, at nearby Tempsford, was a classic example of an over-familiar approach to a day's toil, when 39 year-old Alfred Norman stepped out in front of a ballast train and died instantly.

Two weeks later, this was followed by the demise of 66 year-old Thomas Hill from Great Paxton who was hit and killed by an empty stock train as he was walking to St. Neots along the track, an unhealthy, but common, practice in those days. Although the driver saw Hill he blew a warning whistle but the latter appeared not to hear. It was discovered later that Hill was stone-deaf! Was this another classic case of familiarity breeding contempt, this time for personal safety?

As the four new lines were approaching St. Neots the next stage in the station's evolution came into operation. The buildings and platforms had to be completely remodelled. The old station's 'Down' platform, to Huntingdon, was originally welded on to the main complex which contained the stationmaster's family quarters on the second floor. All this had to be demolished, and a

Fig 51 – Navvies taking a break from back-breaking work.

Fig 52 – Pre-1898 view of the station, with some staff, showing old platform, double-line layout and staggered London platform to left of the lines. Stationmaster (Beavis) and his upper floor home are discernible. The signal is of the GNR 'somersault' type. (Courtesy of David Bushby)

Fig 53 – Detailed study of the station's staff, with stationmaster Mr. Beavis and the shunting horse, 1897. (Courtesy of David Bushby)

Fig 54 – Contractor's engine in 1898 outside the South Goods Shed on Station approach. (Courtesy of David Bushby)

new house built for the stationmaster, before this new head office could be built.

The new house was built, next to Priory Hill Bridge, on the bend at the top of Priory Hill, 300 metres north of the present station, which would have allowed for future expansion of the North goods yard according to railway gossip. Mr. Beavis, the stationmaster, must have felt relieved when he and his family were able to move into this spacious house by August 1898 and away from six months of dust, grime and hassle of construction work which had bedevilled him (see photo P31).

The new 'Up' platform had been ready for use by the end of February although its waiting rooms had to wait until the main building work of the new booking office block and the granary, the largest and most imposing of the new buildings, started in the autumn.

Once the new station layout was in commission, it looked pretty much how it does today. That is, except for the car parks, where the goods depot and sidings were sited, and the footbridge connecting all four platforms with the new station building. All this was too much for one visitor to St. Neots. She had travelled down from London, had not recognised the new architecture, and stayed put in her compartment until she realised her mistake "some stations further". I wonder how many readers have made that mistake or fallen asleep only to be woken by the guard way past the appropriate station.

By October, the new 'slow' train outside-lines were ready for use by the Christmas rush, and a temporary bridge was erected to allow access to the platforms from the new spacious and convenient booking hall. Passengers soon realised how inconvenient this was especially in cold driving precipitation. Ladies were particularly susceptible to this inclement weather with their ankle-length blossomy skirts sitting in a train in drenched clinging folds of textile.

Christmas was a particularly uncomfortable time. Imagine clambering over the

GREAT NORTHERN RAILWAY

ST. NEOTS MARKET

On **THURSDAY, 13th January,** and each succeeding Thursday until further notice, **THIRD CLASS RETURN MARKET TICKETS TO ST. NEOTS** will be issued as under :—

FROM		TIMES OF STARTING.				FARES TO ST. NEOTS AND BACK.	
		a.m.	a.m.	p.m.	p.m.	s.	d.
HUNTINGDON	DEP.	..	10 59	..	1 25	—	9
Offord	,,	..	11 5	..	1 31	—	5
Biggleswade	,,	9 4	..	12 9	..	1	2
Sandy	,,	9 14	..	12 18	..	—	10
Tempsford	,,	9 20	..	12 24	..	—	5
ST. NEOTS	ARR.	9 28	11 12	12 33	1 39		

The tickets will be available for return from St. Neots by any train on day of issue only.

King's Cross Station, January, 1898.

HENRY OAKLEY, General Manager.

Waterlow & Sons Limited, Printers, London Wall, London.

Fig 55 – Area advert handbill attempting to entice people to attend St. Neots Market in mid-winter, 1898. (Courtesy of Norris Museum, St. Ives)

particularly onerous addition to their daily chores constantly having to lug heavy baggage up and down the steps.

There was the case of the disabled lady who arrived from London and had to be carried in a waiting room chair by three men along the platform, across the tracks and out through the goods shed. This dreadfully demeaning situation has been prevalent for over one hundred years and only now, a few months after the national disabilities legislation of 2007, has the decision been made to add lifts to the footbridge – at "some stage"!

The St. Neots Advertiser newspaper, on February 18th 1899, contained an urgent plea that this problem should be discussed with the Great Northern Railway before it caused either an accident or unnecessary antagonism. There was a genuine, if unfounded, fear that some members of the public would find the new arrangements so inconvenient they would patronise other stations in the area rather than St. Neots.

Local opinions were ignored, however, and sections of the new permanent footbridge began to arrive in March 1899. By mid-June the new bridge was in place and the temporary one was removed.

There was still the matter of the wind and rain-swept nature of the new open character

footbridge with wet drapes and struggling with parcels. There was an outcry against the bridge and the local papers took up the mounting campaign for an effective solution to the problem. The porters were having a

Fig 56 – Station footbridge sporting weather roof. (Joe Doncaster Collection)

of the edifice. Something had to be done! The opinion of local townsfolk was to press for a subway but this was flatly refused; I suspect the reason being the permanent footbridge was already under contractual construction. The Town Council then asked the Company to add a roof to the footbridge but the initial request for this was rejected in 1901 on the grounds of expense.

Enter on to the scene that old saying "it's not what you know but who you know" and this applied in this instance. If you cast your mind back to Octavius Wilkinson, his grandson now enters the scene. George Surtees Wilkinson, parliamentary agent living in Aspley Guise adjacent to Woburn, was contacted by St. Neots District Council for his help. It was known he was very friendly with Colonel Frank Shuttleworth, a director of the Great Northern Railway Company.

This approach was partially successful as a footbridge roof was built and placated users to some degree. After half a century the regularly repaired roof, appearing like a patchwork quilt from a distance, lasted until 1949 when it became the target of St. Neots District Council's gaze. The railway had been nationalised the year before and the Council thought, because it had a roof-type structure, they could levy a tax on it in the form of a council rate.

The Railway Executive responded in those austere post-war recession days simply by demolishing the roof claiming it had become unsafe, hence the reason why today's commuters 'enjoy' the delights of our variable weather.

The only problem then rumbling on was the question of rating the new buildings, and a long wrangle ensued between the Town Council and the Company, yet again singling out the new large granary. Before the alterations, the station buildings' rateable value was £469 but the Council wanted to raise it to £500; the Great Northern Company argued there was no justification for any change.

The footbridge remained in this state until 1983. The old 1898 lattice type was inspected around 1980 and a decision to replace it was taken due to its poor state of repair. The impending electrification of the line in 1986 necessitated the rebuild anyway because the old footbridge was too low for accommodating the projected overhead wires. In addition, the wires required a closed parapet style for safety reasons.

This footbridge might be replaced and have lifts added to allow disabled people to use the station instead of having to travel at least ten miles to access rail services.

Sloppy Practice leads to a Consideration of Manslaughter

The completion of track quadrupling in 1898 meant that St. Neots Station and line layout changed out of all recognition. Engine drivers and guards had to become acquainted with the new operating plan or there was potential for disaster particularly in fog or darkness hours.

Nothing is perfect and flaws in any system are likely to be deepened when irregular members of staff are working a shift on a route not totally familiar to them. In those circumstances these people should work in the presence of local employees otherwise health and safety issues become relegated to the dustbin. It is no defence for people to state that they were simply following rules and regulations. We all know they are never watertight or they would not need revising at regular intervals.

Soap-box time over, what triggered off such thoughts? T'was on yet another dark night, on September 13th 1900, twenty months after the last spike had been hammered into the track and the new station buildings had received their last lick of paint.

The 8.38pm 'down' train had just disgorged a fair number of travellers on the 'fast' line platform when the relief driver, Walter Selwood, who was unsure of the new track layout, knew he had to vacate the line his train currently occupied in favour of a scheduled express six or seven miles behind and on the same line. That had to have a clear run. He knew he had to shunt onto another line with the help of signalman Charlie Wilson in the 'north' signal-box.

After the crash, Selwood was heard to say he thought he had shunted backwards onto the 'slow down' line but by the time of the (adjourned) inquest a week later, and once more at the Railway Inn, he went along with the general discussion that it was the siding specially laid for such waiting-shunted refuge incidents. The siding was, in fact, the remnants of the previous 'down' line prior to the 1898 widening construction, and accounts for the present gap between the current station building and the nearest (slow) line.

The inquest heard driver Selwood offer accounts about using platform lamps for guidance over complete clearance off the 'slow' line because the small round trackside disc signals light, no bigger than a florin (an old 10p), was insufficient. He said he was confused because the relevant platform lamps were not lit.

The train guard, William Lodge, said he only worked one week in every month on this line and had never assisted in this manoeuvre at St. Neots so he was also unfamiliar with the process. So, what actually happened?

Behind the engine, the train consisted of 15 vehicles made up of five carriages, a horse box, eight passenger coaches, one carriage brake, one brake van and one empty cattle van. Any sharp-eyed reader worth his or her salt, as they say, can tally that up to a contradictory figure. Quite right, too. The truth was that the train crew had no idea how many vehicles were behind the engine! Their accounts at the Coroner's inquiry varied. After departure from King's Cross the train dropped off and picked up vehicles at Hatfield, Hitchin and Arlesey – and no-one kept an accurate count.

When it came to the reversing shunt at St. Neots the driver did not realise how important the length of his train would be to positioning. The train did reverse too far by a distance of 48 yards (14.5m) albeit at a brisk walking pace. The result was that the empty cattle van on the end hit the non-sprung buffers with a steady force which pushed the van and the preceding guard's brake up into the air to form an inverted V-shape to a height of 30 feet (9m).

In front of the guard's brake was a carriage brake, a vehicle of passenger compartments and a small guard's brake compartment at the rear. When the accident occurred the guard's brake pushed through the wall of what should have been an empty guard's compartment in the carriage brake. Unfortunately, this space was occupied by 62-year old John Jennings, a G.N.R. guard from New England Marshalling Yard at Peterborough. He had taken a goods train to London and was returning home as a passenger, preferring to sit on his own in the guard's space.

The beams of the rear wall of the brake compartment pincered Jennings' head and neck, breaking the latter and cutting the jugular artery. When the compartment was entered by rescuers, blood was dripping out of the carriage onto the track. It was assumed he had died instantly, and was so strongly pinned by the beams his body was not able to be removed until five hours later.

The express due within a few minutes was stopped after the crashed train's guard (who had been sitting in his own compartment instead of observing the reversal in support of the driver) had alerted the signalman. A more serious crash was averted by this prompt action because the incident had cut the support wires to the large, heavy main line signal post which had fallen across the 'fast' lines in the path of the express.

A break-down gang arrived from Peterborough four hours after the accident occurred and got to work immediately before Jennings body was removed. The two upright vehicles were pulled over across three tracks leaving only the far goods line to London open. Mr. Beavis, the stationmaster, piloted all traffic up and down this route for nearly two hours until blocked lines were cleared. This whole incident caused a traffic jam of huge proportions on each side of St. Neots. Once more, many procedural lessons were learnt.

In the same week as this latest fatality, the Countess of Dysart re-appeared at a celebration of her brother's coming-of-age party a mere two miles from the station. At Croxton Hall! Her parents owned the estate and two local villages, Croxton and Eltisley. She presented a silver cup to be played for each year by the two village cricket teams (her brother was killed in the First World War, and I am led to believe the cup is still in existence). It seemed to be an incredible coincidence that the Countess nearly lost her life in the 1895 crash, just down the road from her family home, on a journey that had no relevance to the area.

Working Horses at the Station

Horses have been used on the railways since their invention. Movement of wagons in smaller goods yards up and down the country was an ideal 'pastime' for a horse as its only fuels needed being oats, hay and the occasional pint of beer in the case of the last St. Neots "Charlie" as described later in this section.

St. Neots Station was no exception and the horse was usually named "Charlie", a name common to railway shires. The volume of traffic through the station's yard was so considerable before the First World War two horses were needed. The station had two yards; a larger one to the north, with a premier warehouse-cum-granary, a weighbridge and a crane. There was also a smaller goods yard south of the 'down' (Huntingdon-bound) platform with its own handling shed and weighbridge office.

The horses were taken from 'north' to 'south' whenever the job demanded. Only one horse was needed some time after the Great War. These magnificent Shire horses were used until 1960 at St. Neots and the final "Charlie" is believed, by 'locals', to be the last working shunting horse on the Eastern Region of British Railways. He was transferred to Newmarket Station for a few years until his final job was to shunt his own horse-box, which was used to carry him to glorious retirement to a sanctuary at Clare Hall in Somerset.

Fig 57 – 'Charlie' the shunting horse c.1950 with handler Arthur Payne.
(Courtesy of David Rudd)

The sidings' transfers of horses could be quite dangerous at times. It was on a thick foggy morning, at eight o'clock, on Thursday October 22nd 1904 when shunter Edward Seymour and his assistant Austin Barringer, were shunting two wagons in the 'south' goods yard. Job finished, the two men each led a horse back to the 'north' yard along the 'down'

slow line – in the fog.

Suddenly, a light engine (one with neither wagons nor carriages) hit them. Barringer released his horse immediately and saved himself but Seymour held on to his charge. The two horses were killed instantly one of which was disembowelled. Seymour was knocked down and seriously injured with damage to a foot, concussion and a fractured skull.

In the autumn of 1919 there was a national railway strike. One major consideration of the station staff, who withdrew their labour, was the welfare of the shunting horses. The staff volunteered to feed and exercise the animals until the G.N.R. instructed the men to desist. Ordinary townsfolk, encouraged by the G.N.R., took over these tasks thus giving the horses an unexpected holiday.

The last "Charlie" was stabled at the Station Hotel. At the end of his working day the horse, which was tied to an empty yard rail between jobs, was unhitched and allowed to amble his way back to the stable unaccompanied. He refused to go direct to the Hotel stable yard but preferred to go to the public bar window, tap on it with his head, and wait for a customary pint of ale to be brought out to him. What a way to dispose of the 'slops'!

"Charlie" was transferred to Newmarket Goods Station in 1960, when the Station Hotel was demolished, to join two other shunting horses, "Tommy" and "Butch". The former died of a heart attack in 1961 while at work, and the latter was retired in 1965 leaving "Charlie" to work on alone thus becoming the very last British Railways' shunting horse. He retired on February 21st 1967 to Clare Hall after being the pride of the Wembley Horse of the Year Show in 1965.

Pre-1945 Buses to the Station from the Town Centre

The station, being based a mile outside the town centre, was extremely inconvenient for travellers and merchants alike but, as in all similar circumstances, this became an opportunity for an entrepreneur to earn extra cash.

The Market Square situation of the Cross Keys Hotel provided its proprietors with a golden opportunity to buy a horse-drawn omnibus (known as a 'horse bus'). They created, at least as early as 1852, a service which claimed to meet every passenger train that stopped at St. Neots whether there were any passengers or not. Its patronage was very slow in building up possibly partly due to the fact that the coach was "one of the most disagreeable in every respect" in England.

Oh, for the joy of anticipating being pampered by a coach-ride to and from the station before an arduous third class journey to London through the tunnels south of Hitchin! Some horse bus journeys were so overcrowded that a second, and smaller, horse bus was bought to accompany the main one. You are always reminded that you should be prepared for the worst when working with animals and this horse bus service saw its catalogue of accidents, none of which were fatal. Some of these accidents could have given Buster Keaton and Charlie Chaplin ideas for film scripts.

On one occasion, in October 1875, the driver was 'rooting' for some luggage when an engine whistle startled the two horses. Off they bolted, gaining speed down Station Road, along Cambridge Street, High

Fig 58 – The 'taxi service' at the station in 1899 after quadrupling and before the footbridge acquired its roof. (Courtesy of Norris Museum St Ives)

Fig 59 – The 'yellow-peril' charabanc which plied between the Cross Keys Hotel, Market Square and the Station. Jim Sawford was the driver. (Courtesy of Barry Mills)

Street and into the Market Square. The two passengers were shaken but otherwise not harmed and justified in boasting they were joint holders of a new speed record. A fortnight later the horse bus had just delivered George Bower to his door when the driver attempted too sharp a turn and the whole contraption toppled over. On another journey one of the horses collapsed and died.

There was a period when the station bus horses were used to haul the town's fire engine on emergencies. Imagine the passengers' consternation when, on one occasion, the horses were in demand, to tackle a fire, in the middle of one of the scheduled journeys leaving all and sundry stranded on Cambridge Road with their luggage.

In July 1914 fossil fuel replaced hay-driven coaches for luggage-free passengers, however, when Miss Cranstone, the Cross Keys landlady, bought a charabanc. The horses and coach were kept for people with bulky packages but dispensed with in 1920 when a new motor-bus was bought much to the delight of townsfolk. This service continued until the 1940s.

Railway Schemes to the Town Centre

Believe it or not, three schemes were proposed between 1895 and 1920. There was a major problem in the town. The main industries were either in the town centre or spread along both banks of this delightful riverside settlement, but the railway station was one mile due east. This busy station's link, the Cambridge road, had become the umbilical cord sustaining its new energetic endeavour.

The heavy traffic, however, took its huge toll on the road's health. Deep ruts and potholes were imposing exasperating frustrations on traders in particular. Something had to be done, and the initiative was led by the owners of the town centre industries.

They became member councillors in the newly created Urban District Council structure so as to keep a finger on the pulse of the town's industrial wealth and jobs.

The first scheme they planned was the 1895 gasworks railway, which was sited opposite the present-day Peacock's Auction Rooms adjacent to The Common.

Many people in St. Neots kept a mental note of this 1895 idea and it was taken to heart by High Street clothier Arthur Norris in 1902. He displayed an excellent understanding and awareness of the town's trade and transport situation at the time of the main line's opening in 1850, what was needed half a century later, and how to raise the interest of the G.N.R. in the idea.

Arthur Norris's long life experienced the heady earliest days of the station which attracted a huge eruption of trade opportunities. He stated publicly that George Bower's factory was going strong in 1850 and they were carting fifty tons of iron products a mile to and from the station every day! Other traders to benefit were the local farmers, merchants and market gardeners, the last being in one of the most important soil areas in England for growing vegetables. Many tons of local hay were being delivered by farmers for transporting up to King's Cross for feeding to the city's horses. The future looked very bright indeed.

Arthur calculated that the station's distance from the town was sufficient to cost George Bower enough extra cash that would have paid for a branch line into the Market Square. In addition, he intimated that traders using the station during the last fifty years had incurred, at a low estimate, a quarter of a million pounds of transport costs just to and from the goods yards.

A major feature in Arthur's argument was the distance of the station from the town centre. The station is at the end of a mile-long very gentle rise away from the river and town centre ending in a fairly sharp gradient for 200 metres up Station Road to the goods yards. Imagine being a horse confronted with the prospect of pulling a cart full of beer or flour, especially before permanent paving had been installed. Arthur calculated that, in horse-energy miles, the return journey was equal to a four mile trek.

Traction means also occupied Arthur's mind. He reckoned that a small shunter would cost a mere £3 a day, could work in the goods yards, and the two shunting horses could be sold and thus save on feed.

Next on his agenda was passenger traffic. The proposed branch light railway would attract yet more passengers, in his estimation. He said that St. Neots was the "prettiest town" in the whole G.N.R. system and the Great Eastern, London & North Western and Midland companies had nothing to compare on their lines within fifty miles of London. That one is a bit of a tall order to stand up to modern scrutiny but he was not far off the mark. At least, Arthur made a point; today, it is a fine riverside market town. He was trying to entice well-heeled executives to consider living in St. Neots and using the train to commute southwards. If only he could see the mad scramble at the station at the rush hours today!

Arthur's final discussion shot was an attempt to push the Urban District Council into contacting three of the G.N.R.'s new top executives, Mr. W. Grinling (chief goods traffic manager), Mr. J. Proud (Superintendent of the Line) and Mr. G. Shaw (goods manager) whose careers he knew a great deal about. He wanted them to be invited to the town to discuss the chances of a branch line along Cambridge Road and the High Street.

All this deliberation came to nothing, but the whole idea did show considerable flair. Competitive pressure was mounting on the G.N.R. with contemporary strong rumours abounding about a branch line being planned to Eaton Socon from Sandy's Girtford Bridge (c/o L.&N.W.R.).

Further schemes included one to the Tan Yard near today's Navigation Wharf in Eynesbury suburb. This was planned to be a branch down Duck Lane and to the river to service that artery's industries such as the Jordan & Addington seed factory, farms, Tebbutt's timber yard, the important Little Paxton paper mill and other industries in the town centre.

The final attempt was as late as 1920 when the town centre idea was resurrected by the industrialists and councillors yet again. This time, a five-strong deputation was sent to see the Transport Minister in Whitehall but nothing came of it. By this time advancements in lorry design proved to be an excellent alternative and truncated any further thoughts in this direction.

Paine's Brewing & Milling Company trading through the Station warehouse in 1900

James Paine & Co. relied almost totally upon St. Neots Station's existence for its trade. The company was a central pivot in the region buying great amounts of grain from farms and merchants around the U.K., Europe and the New World. The G.N.R. transported grain from Eastern England in particular, and their dock facilities at King's Lynn and Boston dealt with the main European imports from Denmark and the Russian steppes. By the end of the Nineteenth Century the traditional suppliers were under enormous price competition from the New World (South Australia, American Prairies, Argentinian Pampas) so Paine's began to import wheat and barley through London Docks, especially Millwall and Poplar). A sample from 1894 is:-

Jan 13th "Peterston" East Millwall 200 sacks of wheat

Feb 21st "Mendl" East Millwall 10 sacks of barley

Feb 22nd "Peterston" East Millwall 105 sacks of wheat

Mar 5th "Trumian" East Millwall 112 sacks of barley

Mar 9th "Caffila" East Millwall 100 sacks of wheat

'Sacks' = bushels (60lbs for wheat; 48lbs for barley)

Wheat and barley were unloaded from goods vans and trucks at the station goods yard warehouse in sacks and transported either to the, now conserved, flour mill building, which had exquisite mahogany chutes, in Bedford Street on the northern edge of the town adjacent to the gasworks. This facility allowed the company to dominate the processing of the grain which was in high demand throughout the U.K. The wheat was milled into a series of flour products and the barley went down the road of brewing.

When all the processing in the two

Fig 60 – North Goods Yard granary and main warehouse, circa 1912. (Courtesy of Judith Addington)

factories had been finished, and the products were in their prime condition, orders flowed, packed and then dispatched to the station. These products included:-

Malt extract, malt flour, germ barley, baking flour, "John Bull" ales, broad bran, biscuit flour, wheat-meal, semolina, 'Silver Spray' (for separating the suspensions, or finings, in the beer), empty bags (500 each time) and even sacks of potatoes.

Record keeping was adhered to keenly, and the analysis of a pad of an incredible 182 dispatch delivery sheets for December 2nd to 31st 1901 highlighted 51 destinations ranging from Exeter, Bradford, Lowestoft, Windsor, Manchester, Hastings and several to Gibraltar via 'Shed no. 12, Royal Albert Dock, London. By far the most regular destination was the King's Cross Granary near the station, which seemed to be the Capital's storage depot for the G.N.R. Many of the products were for smaller breweries and many of the notes had "very urgent" prominently displayed probably due to the proximity of Christmas.

One order was from Toronto, Canada and was for two tons of malt flour and 28 pounds of malt extract. The order left the station for Boston, Lincolnshire, one of the G.N.R's primary ports, and was loaded on to the "S.S. Bostonian" which was bound for (yes, you've guessed it) Boston, Massachusets! A further search on the history of this steamer showed that it had to steam through the Grand Banks Sea area off Newfoundland, notorious for its fogs. It was 18 months after the Paine's malt extract and flour voyage that the ship scraped the barnacles off its keel by colliding with an iceberg in dense fog on July 15th 1903, Titanic-style, and survived.

The object of this little dispatch analysis 'window' is to emphasise the importance of the goods yards to the industrial activity of a classic agricultural market town at that time, and before the arrival of the goods lorry. Out of 25 trading days a total of 353 tons of Paine's processed goods went through the railway warehouse, thus hinting at how much raw grain was arriving.

Paine's brewery and mill complex was only one of two large breweries in the town so that suggests that a much greater tonnage passed through the warehouse's books. Another equally important company, similarly occupied, was the Priory site of Jordan & Addington's brewery along with their water mill two miles distant at Eaton Socon. They displayed their prominence by displaying their name on the station warehouse as seen in the following illustration taken just before the First World War.

St. Neots Entertains London's Great Northern Railway employees

It may surprise the reader that St. Neots attempted to develop a day tourist trade one hundred years ago. The somewhat charming Market Place was supported by the nearby River Great Ouse attractions and the "Health Spa" waters based at Samuel Jones Paper Mill at Little Paxton. Mr. F Beeson built a few boats one of which was a pleasure steamer named "Cosy" which plied its pleasure cruises along the river.

Mr. Beeson contacted the G.N.R. in London and they jumped at the chance to entertain their loyal employees to a day out in St. Neots! Three trips were organised on successive Saturdays in June 1907. On the second trip, forty of the G.N.R.'s King's

Cross Stationery Department plucked up courage to visit this unheard-of attraction but their judgment, to 'test the waters' so delighted them, resulted in many "Cosy" trips up and down the river. Lunch was taken in the Cross Keys Hotel followed by a cricket match on The Common between the G.N.R. Stationery Department and St. Neots Harmonic! Who called the tune?

The next day, the successful visit was repeated with the G.N.R. King's Cross Parcel Department, with 55 employees indulging in these delights. This time, the cricket match was between 'Married v Single' teams. Forget your corporate golf days and boxes at Premiership sporting events; come to glorious St. Neots for a day out on the river!

It is not known how successful the campaign was at attempting to attract tourists to this riverside town, and to imbibe the health-nurturing natural spring waters of nearby Little Paxton village.

The G.N.R. placarded 300 of their stations for several years with posters portraying and, hopefully, enticing day-trippers to this pleasant relaxing market town with its watering holes. Ah, those were the days when St. Neots boasted about its attractions, with the help of the railway company, from Doncaster and King's Lynn down to King's Cross and St. Albans.

Another Fatal Local Accident

It was in late May, 1912 that the driver of G.N.R. engine number 12 noticed a shockingly mutilated body at Skew Bridge, Great Paxton, and spread for fifty yards along the 'up' line at 4 a.m. on the Thursday morning. The driver reported the incident to Signalman Ashley at Great Paxton signal-box, about one and a half miles north of St. Neots Station. At 4.24 a.m., the driver of engine number 755 saw the body, stopped and moved it into the six foot way, this time reporting it to the new shift signalman Bryant.

The police were informed, and the body was removed to the Station Hotel at St. Neots Station, there to await the inquest at 11 a.m. one day later. The body's clothes' pockets were searched for identity clues, and two pieces of paper pinpointed a 64 year old William Mayes from Wilby, near Wellingborough and his son Frank from Huntingdon.

It was obvious from the injuries that William had been walking along the line and had been hit by an engine at some time in the night. The greater part of the head had been completely torn away, both his arms were severed from the body and his legs were very badly crushed, one of his boots being completely torn off. His facial features were unrecognisable. It is not wise to argue with an engine!

It appears that William, according to his son, suffered from absent-mindedness and loss of memory. He had wandered off from his home on the previous Monday, had called at his distant relative Frederick Mayes, a Kimbolton greengrocer, before walking off to the St. Ives Workhouse for a Tuesday night bed. He was seen at Kisby's Hut, Papworth Everard at 8 p.m. the day before his accident. If he was homeward-bound he could well have been attempting to cross the river at St. Neots and was using the railway as the quickest way to the town's bridge. This incident, recorded as "death by misadventure", highlights the danger of walking along any railway track.

The Great Northern Railway's part in saving Kimbolton School in 1913

Mr. Matthews, of Biddenham, Bedford, contacted me on November 24th 2005 regarding my Kimbolton railway book. The conversation progressed to discuss Kimbolton School and its predecessor, the Grammar School.

In 2010, Mr. Matthews died aged about 90 years, and used to live in Gt. Staughton many years go. His grandfather became stationmaster at Grafham but before that he had been a blacksmith in Gt. Staughton, five miles west of St. Neots. Mr. Matthews then went on to describe how his grandfather saved the day over the financial health of Kimbolton Grammar School in 1913.

Mr. Ingram was headmaster then. In that year he was told by accountants the school would go bankrupt if he didn't do something immediately about the school's debts. He arranged a bridging loan with a London bank which required a visit to London for negotiation and possible signing.

Mr. Ingram was motoring through Gt. Staughton on his way to St Neots Station to catch the London train when his car broke down. He was close by Mr. Matthews' blacksmith's shop. He had a motorbike with sidecar and volunteered to take Mr. Ingram to the station.

When they got to St Neots River Bridge Mr. Ingram asked Mr. Matthews to stop at the Barclays Bank on the left just after the Bridge Hotel because he was desperate for ready cash for the day. Mr. Ingram emerged from the bank but dropped a £1 note in the gutter. Mr. Ingram told his saviour-driver not to bother with it because they were late for the train.

Arriving on the London-bound platform just as the train was about to leave, someone spotted Mr. Ingram's agitated haste and flung open a carriage door, thus saving the day. If he had missed it the deal would have been in jeopardy and the school would have been forced to close.

Mr. Matthews went back to the Market Place and found the £1 note still in the gutter. He returned it to Mr. Ingram at the school a few days later whereupon Mr. Ingram immediately offered free places for his sons to attend the School! £1 in those days was nearly equivalent to a week's labouring wages.

First World War

The Great War of 1914-18 had a serious effect on the operation of Britain's railway network. Engines, wagons and coaches were badly needed to ferry troops, ordnance and animals to the Channel ports. Fares were substantially increased and the amount of luggage allowed was reduced. All this activity had to be co-ordinated sensibly and efficiently. Regiments and ordnance, travelling from the north, required uninterrupted streamlined travel to the Channel ports, and the Government created a type of 'British Railways' bureaucracy to combine these movements otherwise there would have been chaos (there were about 250 independent railway companies in 1912). This structure gave the railway companies a 'taste' of the efficiency benefits this type of co-operation could bring to all.

Journeys to and from London, for St. Neots people, were disrupted by the national urgent need for other trains to take precedence on the bottleneck of the double-line Welwyn Viaduct. This led to up to an additional two hours en route. To make matters worse, there was no middle-of-the-day service from St. Neots to London for over four hours. Passengers accepted this stoically in a patriotic spirit especially when the war fatality figures began to hit home hard. Despite all of this, and in some of the darkest days of the War, many day-trippers poured through St. Neots Station to sample the town's delights at Whitsun in 1917.

Fig 61 – A busy early autumn scene in 1917 at the station dispatching hay and straw for the trenches on the Western Front. (Courtesy of David Bushby)

You must remember that, although this was the first war in which the combustion engine played a significant part, most of the ordnance, food and equipment were transported near the front by horsepower. In the provision of straw and hay for this aspect of the war effort, St. Neots Station became an important centre for the dispatch of these vital equine victuals for horses and mules. One of the finest photographs of it, taken one Saturday morning in 1917, shows the station yard brimming with army personnel and new War Department traction engines which had heaved and wheezed wagons up the Station Road incline laden with bales of straw from local farms ready for loading into waiting railway trucks. The local Army Commander in charge of the operation is seen as passenger in his 1911 Daimler 12-horse power 4-seater car (reg. no. BM3876).

There was great disruption to rail traffic at St. Neots Station on the 24th January 1917 with the London-bound lines being disrupted for nearly three hours. At about half past five in the dark part of the afternoon, a goods train comprising eighty loaded wagons drawn by two engines, heading for King's Cross, started off on the main line after a compulsory stop while waiting the next section to clear of traffic. The sudden jerk created by the two engines caused a coupling to break three wagons from the brake van thus stranding four vehicles.

Near Abbotsley Road Bridge yet another break occurred, this time leaving behind another fifty wagons. The train guard asked the St. Neots signalman to warn the two-mile-distant Little Barford signalman to stop the train, now with only twenty wagons remaining.

One of the engines had to steam all the way to Tempsford Station, three miles to the south, where it was able to transfer tracks to return to St. Neots. The engine then pushed all the incriminating wagons forward to the front section. The train, now complete once more, started off on the main line after blocking it for those three hours and sending expresses shamefully down the slow goods line. A subsequent inspection showed the breakage was probably caused by the effect of the cold weather on the metal couplings.

Two poignant human stories help to illustrate the enormous mental stresses that this stagnant rigor mortis-ridden war had inflicted on the trench soldier. In May 1916, a soldier was found lying injured on the railway line four miles north of St. Neots and near to Offord. Upon his discovery, it wasn't clear what had happened but, after his recovery, it transpired that he was returning from the trenches to his home in Durham. He claimed he had been used to the slow trains of France and he had panicked because he thought the train was going too fast and would crash. So, he jumped off!

Desertion was an ongoing problem, especially after the carnage of the Somme and Paschendale. In another incident, a soldier under escort jumped from a speeding train close to the town station in an attempt to escape, but he was killed outright.

The Growing Influence of Trade Unionism

According to David Bushby, the prime St. Neots' historian, during the Nineteenth Century the G.N.R. management had been able to run the company without too many disgruntled demands from its workforce (cast your mind back to September 1875 and the chapter entitled "Short Change for Sunday Duty on Railways" at the 'Belmont

Tavern', London). Such rumblings had generally proved to be ineffective. All this was to change dramatically in the Twentieth Century as trade unionism and worker power began to exert their influences.

Until the First World War the horse was the main 'engine-room' of local city transport. Hay was sucked into London in railway wagons like an autonomic peristaltic action and the G.N.R. was a major player in this field of commerce. This resulted in a major problem; heaps of steaming manure accumulated which were lovingly collected by city entrepreneurs and sold back to rural agents for the farmers to spread on their fields. St. Neots tended to deal with a dealer in London's Blackwall district. He prepared wagonloads for the G.N.R.'s daily "Dung Train" which supplied the local goods yards.

Way back in 1866, when the national great Cattle Plague (rinderpest) was at its height, unscrupulous dealers ridded themselves of infected beasts by butchering them into small chunks and hiding them in the dung wagons despite the nationwide movement ban on animals, afflicted or otherwise. This culpable action helped sponsor the spread of the disease for a number of years but probably led to St. Neots dealing with just one or two reputable distributors.

This set the scene for the national railway strike in August 1911. The scene in London's rail termini turned ugly at times and the Government was worried about an attempted revolution. London's food supplies were strike-bound in warehouses, and horse-drawn covered food wagons were escorted out of the King's Cross warehouses through narrowing angry lines of strikers. St. Neots, however, was unaffected and trains ran through the station as normal, driven by volunteer labour; the goods yard remained open for trade such as it was.

The next year, however, saw the miners' strike of 1912 which led to massive coal shortages. During March and April many local trains had to be suspended. Local farmers and market gardeners were also badly affected with their reliance upon steam traction engines. The Dung Train service to St. Neots was suspended which led to farmers becoming worried about their soil condition for the next harvest.

An important change came in October 1913 when the G.N.R. employees at the station formed a branch of the National Union of Railwaymen, a clear sign of the growing influence of trade unionism in the area. This gave the railway workers a voice in a way they never had before, and they were soon to use it. As the First World War began to exert an influence on basic commodity prices the St. Neots railway workers, like their counterparts elsewhere, met to discuss the situation and, as a result, sent a resolution to Prime Minister Asquith and the local Member of Parliament, Conservative John Cator. National concerns about the war meant the resolution fell on stony ground.

After the War there was real anxiety about wages not keeping up with rises in the cost of living and this led to the great national railway strike of September and October 1919, an event denounced by both politicians and, not surprisingly, the press (still right-wing) as unpatriotic and the work of anarchists. After all, people in power were looking over their shoulders for 'Reds-under-the-beds'; it was only two years after the start of the Communist Revolution in Russia. The only occasion when tanks were deployed on to the streets of the United Kingdom to quell a strike was during this confrontation which occurred in Glasgow.

The whole of St. Neots Station staff supported the strike, with the exception of two men, leaving Stationmaster Gayton with many problems, the solutions to some of which may appear strange, even dangerous and totally unacceptable and confrontational today.

The strike began in the most bizarre September weather experienced in the 20th Century! The month began with a welcome 'Indian Summer' which rapidly turned into a heat wave with September record-breaking 32'C temperatures. Fine for the farmers but these balmy conditions deteriorated rapidly when the wind 'backed' in from the north to blanket the country in snow, the earliest recorded fall ever in St. Neots. The goods yard activities, already seriously curtailed, ground to a complete halt until the thaw occurred two days later.

Mr. Gayton's first concern was for the voluminous quantity of perishable goods which were in the goods–yard and awaiting distribution. His first task was to contact the intended recipients and arranged for them to collect if and when it was convenient. Mr. Lynn, with a new motor lorry, was a great help here, and delivered a number of consignments for people. This was a massive time-consuming and energy-sapping exer-cise at the time, but it was well worth the effort for eighty of the ninety eight wagons in the two yards, excluding trucks of coal, were cleared by volunteers.

The Stationmaster's 'beefy' daughter took charge of communications by pulling the heavy levers in St. Neots North signal-box while the South box was closed down completely for the duration of the strike. A few trains did run, with the aid of non-union labour and managers, despite the strike, and the Company eventually arranged an emergency timetable. There was, however, no proper signalling, so trains had to proceed in places at snail's pace.

Inevitably, many local businesses were affected by the disruption to normal trade. Many employers, such as the Paper Mill, Paine's Brewery, and Jordan & Addington found their distribution services badly restricted as there were only a limited number of lorries available to carry goods out of the locality.

Even so, the Great North Road through Eaton Socon was considerably busier than usual. Postal services were affected with only a local delivery operating. The coal yard at the station, however, remained a hive of activity, and local merchants had adequate supplies of the black gold. The Gas Company also had sufficient stock in hand to keep the town supplied with coke, gas and other by-products to alleviate hardship.

This strike precipitated people into adapting to these extreme circumstances by buying war surplus motorized transport, and was probably the first crack in the railway company's near-monopoly on goods transport. This, in turn, may have been the initial trigger leading to the gradual erosion of the volume of railway transport between the two world wars.

The dispute was settled eventually with the strikers squeezing out an agreement on the level of wages that guaranteed them the fair standard of living they had been seeking. A delighted St. Neots Trades Council convened a special meeting to formally thank Mr. J. H. Thomas and the railway union's executive on the splendid fight they had fought for trade unionism and securing such a positive settlement for the employees.

Chapter Four

The London & North Eastern Railway Times

The Absorption of the Great Northern Railway into the L. & N.E.R.

It was stated on an earlier page there were 250 independent railway companies in 1912. At the time, rapid amalgamation was taking place and, by the outbreak of the Great War of Empires in the August of 1914 there were eighty together with a similar number of main lines.

The benefit of experiencing the joint running of this jigsaw of a national railway system during the First World War taught the Government the effectiveness of mutual co-operation between the various companies. Although nationalisation was a totally unpalatable word for the capitalistic society of the United Kingdom, it was obvious to everyone, including the railway companies, something had to be enacted. The result of all the deliberations was the "Rationalisation of Railways Act" of August 19th 1921 which came into force at midnight on January 1st 1923.

Apart from a few short-lined and small railway companies, the Government used this legislation to bring about the famous Grouping of railway companies into four major corporate undertakings lovingly known in railway circles today as the Southern, Great Western, London, Midland & Scottish, and the London & North Eastern (L. & N.E.R.) Railways. You will see, even with a cursory glance at these names, that regional 'kingdoms' had been created and these were to become the 'communal' template for the nationalisation plan twenty five years later.

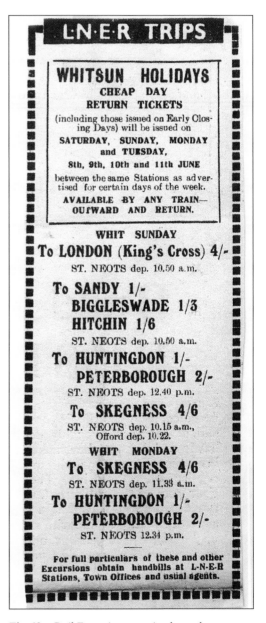

Fig 62 – Rail Excursions remained popular amongst town-folk during L. & N.E.R. times.

(source - St. Neots Advertiser)

The L. & N.E.R. came into existence with the merging of eight major companies which stretched from London to Inverness, Mallaig, Wrexham and almost exclusively in the north-east of England, Lincolnshire and East Anglia.

The creation of the L.& N.E.R. involved the amalgamation of the railway companies grandly titled the North Eastern, Great Central, Hull & Barnsley (to G.C.R. in 1922), Great Eastern, North British, Great North of Scotland and the Great Northern plus 26 minor companies within its sphere of major influence such as the Stamford & Essendine, Nottingham & Grantham Railway & Canal and Nottingham Suburban Railway companies.

Two large pre-Grouping and jointly-owned networks, the Midland & Great Northern and Cheshire Lines Committee continued in L. & N.E.R. and L.M.S. joint ownership under an independent committee. St. Neots railway station, being owned by the G.N.R., became part of the new L. & N.E.R. empire.

Rural Telephones on Railways to help farmers

The general idea of the introduction of telephones and Internet services for the benefit of railway patrons, by railway companies in recent years, is not the result of a modern brain-storming session.

A very interesting scheme of co-operation between farmers and the L. & N.E.R. was activated in January 1926. It involved the installation of Post Office telephone 'instruments' at all rural area stations and this included St. Neots. The Company conceived the idea of inducing farmers to install telephone links between home and their nearest station so they could keep in constant communication with the movements of prices in the market in stock, produce and provisions.

In this way, farmers would be saved considerable time and many ineffective journeys for enquiries. Doubtless, the L. & N.E.R. was privately concerned about the gradual loss of trade to road transport, and this was one way in which the Company was attempting to keep hold of its customers. There were hopes for the scheme to be spread nationwide if it proved to be successful; whether this was the case is not known. Only centenarian farmers could tell you.

The 1926 National General Strike

In the first half of the 1920s the general blue-collar working population became disgruntled with rising inflation and their low wages. It was felt more keenly in the coalmining industry where conditions had deteriorated badly as had relations between the miners and the coalmine owners.

Negotiations between the miners' unions and the owners fell on stony ground to such an extent that the Trades Union Congress (founded c.1877) intervened and officially called out the miners on the Congress's first National Strike in early May 1926. It became known as the "General Strike" once workers in other industries decided to join the protest.

The Strike incorporated so many key workers in various industries it had an immediate effect on St. Neots people, industry, commerce and farming. Everyday goods deliveries were badly affected due to the still very heavy reliance upon the Station's goods yard.

The yard's closure affected everything from coal deliveries to milk supplies and fresh food and, as the withdrawal of labour involved so many workers in the dispersal of national news down to grassroots local level, strike news was not distributed in the normal accepted fashion of the day. Radio news bulletins did their best and newspaper proprietors, like The Times, strived to print daily two-sided foolscap sheets retailing at a grossly inflated two old pence (today, less than 1p). The Daily Mail was the first paper to suspend publication while the T.U.C. immediately began to publish its very own strike bulletin called the British Worker.

The L. & N.E.R. produced its very own most informative company daily newspaper which kept a tally on the number of its employees either returning to work or refusing to strike, and the total of running trains on the company's daily timetable.

St. Neots townsfolk relied heavily on the railway station's services despite the proximity and growing influence of the nearby Great North Road for lorry transport half a mile to the west of the river. The town's gasworks, based on the northern edge of the town at the entrance to The Common, had anticipated the Strike's potential disruption to coal supplies, essential for local gas production by heating coal in enclosed chambers, and the company announced at the Strike's onset that it had stockpiles for several weeks.

On Day One of the General Strike (May 4th) only one train called at St. Neots disgorging one passenger. The usual bustle of the goods yard, with its regular 70-80 wagons, ground to a halt. Out of the dozen or so station employees only four non-

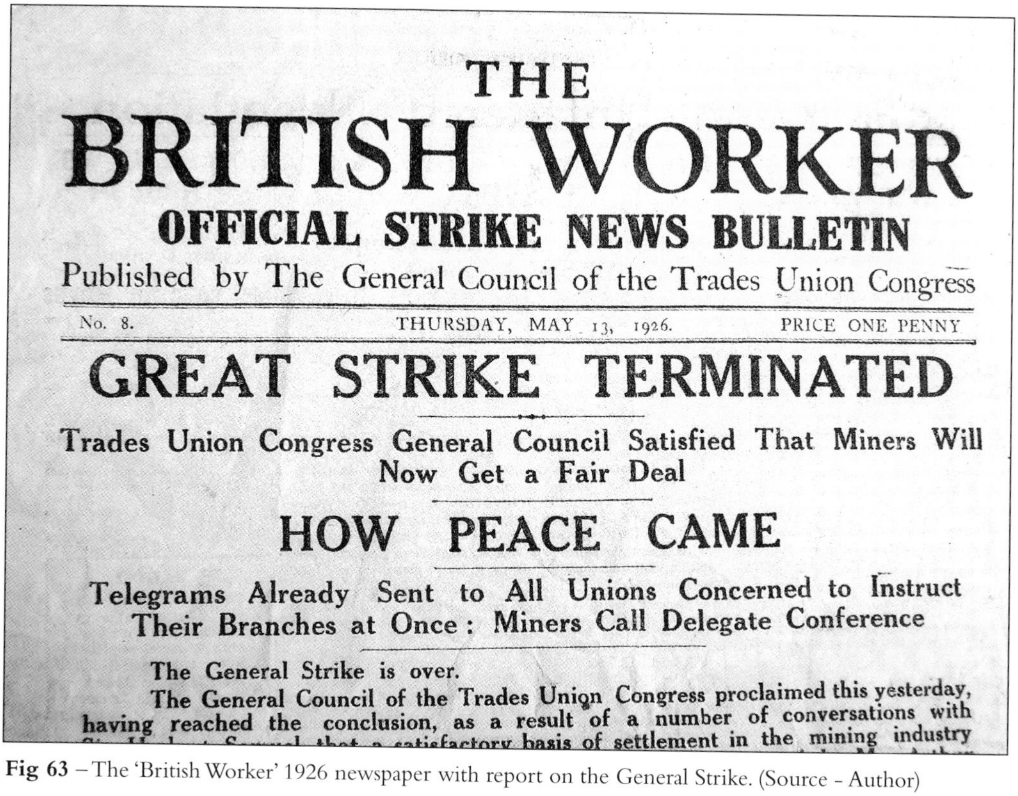

THE BRITISH WORKER

OFFICIAL STRIKE NEWS BULLETIN

Published by The General Council of the Trades Union Congress

No. 8.   THURSDAY, MAY 13, 1926.   PRICE ONE PENNY

GREAT STRIKE TERMINATED

Trades Union Congress General Council Satisfied That Miners Will Now Get a Fair Deal

HOW PEACE CAME

Telegrams Already Sent to All Unions Concerned to Instruct Their Branches at Once : Miners Call Delegate Conference

The General Strike is over.

The General Council of the Trades Union Congress proclaimed this yesterday, having reached the conclusion, as a result of a number of conversations with ... that a satisfactory basis of settlement in the mining industry ...

Fig 63 – The 'British Worker' 1926 newspaper with report on the General Strike. (Source - Author)

union members refused to join the Strike. These men agreed to feed and exercise the goods yard's horses.

Perishable foods were the most vulnerable to the rail disruption. Gone was the immediate means of transport to London's dairies for milk, and the fish trains (from the East Coast ports) ceased to run. Fish wagons, strike-bound in London's goods yards, became easy to identify especially if the casual visitor happened to be down-wind of the offending conveyance!

It was vital that supplies should trickle through to the British Empire's capital and its burgeoning hordes of workers and their families. These ever-inventive Anglo-Saxon Brits began to adapt remarkably quickly despite reports of serious crowd disturbances emanating from Hammersmith, Hackney, Chiswick and Poplar. Alternative food transport methods had to be devised pronto.

Instead of farmers' milk being sent each day to the Station yard the churns were accumulated in the town's Market Square for loading on to lorries. The increased transport cost saw the price of milk escalate overnight by one old penny a pint. Lowestoft's fish trade continued to operate now by road. Eighty tons were dispatched on the first day of the Strike but the increased costs caused fish prices to double in London's Billingsgate Fish Market and, by Wednesday, this had swollen to a mighty 400 tons on the day.

Postal services were seriously disrupted; stranded sacks of letters were 'rescued' and sent ahead by road. People were implored not to try and send any packages or letters over eight ounces in weight (225grms.) except for local delivery once a day (as opposed to the usual three deliveries).

An emergency St. Neots Urban District Council's committee was created, like those all around the country, and volunteers were urged to sign up to maintain essential services such as food supply and transport. On Wednesday May 5th, the response from volunteers in London was overwhelming with 5,000 registering for training. This brought the total to 12,500 for the past two days, and this pattern was repeated around the country. One of the St. Neots' committee's first duties was to take legal action against any local traders if committee members were 'tipped off' about non-essential price increases and profiteering.

Driving licences were required from eligible volunteers, courtesy of the 1903 Driving Licence Act, but these were legally issued until 1930 by the Town Council! Problem solved; a day's instruction on gear changing, steering and basic highway-code rules paved the way for letting loose this maniacal horde of newly qualified drivers on the nation's roads.

The tremendous build-up of volunteers meant that more trains were run after essential instruction and practical training on becoming drivers, firemen, guards and ticket clerks. On Tuesday May 4th two passenger trains called at the Station, one up and one down the line. By Thursday May 6th, less than one week into the strike, one passenger train left for London (at 11.40am) while three arrived from King's Cross (at 11.27am, 3pm, and 5.28pm). Passengers were almost as rare as hen's teeth. Only one person boarded each of the first two trains while no-one arrived.

The same day, milk trains resumed their liquid transfer to London from St. Neots. A similar type of train left Stafford L. & N.E.R. for Derby Friargate, Nottingham

L.N.E.R. NEWS.

Printed and Published by the LONDON AND NORTH EASTERN RAILWAY.
Headquarters Office: KING'S CROSS, LONDON, N. 1.

No. 1.   MAY 8th, 1926.   GRATIS

TRAIN INFORMATION.

MAIN LINE.
The principal trains for today,
Sat. May 8th from the three Main
Line Stations are as follows:-
LIVERPOOL STREET
To Cambridge & Norwich Thorpe 9 am.
" Ipswich & Norwich Thorpe 10 am.
" Ipswich & Yarmouth   1 pm.
" Cambridge   11.50 am. & 3.30 pm.
KING'S CROSS
To York (Restaurant Car)   9 am.
" Edinburgh (Restaurant Car) 10 am.
" Peterborough   3 pm.
York to King's Cross   9 am.
Peterborough to King's Cross   9 am.
MARYLEBONE
To Manchester   9.30 am.
" Nottingham   10.10 am.
" Manchester   11.30 am.
" Leicester via Aylesbury 3.25 pm.
Nottingham to Marylebone   4 pm.
Manchester "   " 9.30am. 12 noon.
Leicester "   "   8.50 am.
Liverpool St to Parkeston Quay (Con-
tinental Restaurant Express 7 pm.

---

550 SIGNALMEN ARE AT WORK ON THE L.N.E.R.

There are several V.C.'s amongst the
volunteer engine drivers at Kings Cross.

The Emergency Schedule will remain in
operation until further notice but additional trains will be added as the hours
pass.

No more volunteers are needed at Stratford
until Monday except Signalmen.

The Milk train from Stafford to London
yesterday brought 3500 Churns of milk.

The latest train services are being ex-
hibited daily on the windows of the
L.N.E.R. Receiving Offices throughout
London.

So many letters have been received by the
L.N.E.R. from volunteers offering service
that whilst the Company are most grateful
they find it impossible to send answers
immediately.

NEWS FROM ALL QUARTERS.

650 TRAINS RUNNING
The L.N.E.R. are successfully carrying
out the improved Emergency Schedules of
trains to which the public are rapidly
accustoming themselves and trains are
leaving fully loaded. On Thursday the
L.N.E.R. worked 578 trains and yesterday over 500 were operated.
SPLENDID SERVICE OF VOLUNTEERS
Thousands of volunteers are now being
employed and their efforts are splendid
in the extreme. Sessions at the special
schools for training are continuous and
the position generally shows increasing
activity in all departments.
THE FLYING SCOTSMAN
The main line services have been considerably speeded up, the "FLYING
SCOTSMAN" is now being worked daily
both from King's Cross to Edinburgh and
in the reverse direction Edinburgh to
King's Cross.
HOOK OF HOLLAND ROUTE TO REOPEN
The L.N.E.R. Royal Mail Route from
London to Harwich and the Hook of
Holland every week day will be re-
opened today, May 8th, the boat train
leaving Liverpool Street for Parkeston
Quay at 7.0. p.m. Return services from
the Hook of Holland will commence every
week day from Monday next, May 10th,
arriving at Liverpool Street 10.40. am.
The 7.0. p.m. train from Liverpool
Street tomorrow, Saturday, will also
convey passengers to the motorship
"PARKESTON" leaving Harwich, Parkeston
Quay, on Saturday evening for Esbjerg.
MILK TRAINS AND FOOD WAGONS
In addition to the usual milk trains
which are all working, 313 wagons of
food-stuffs were unloaded at the
L.N.E.R. London depots yesterday, and
an emergency depot for bacon and pork
has been opened on No. 10 platform at
Liverpool Street Station.
POTATOES FOR LONDON
Trains of potatoes have been run from
Cambridge, Boston, and Spalding dis-
tricts to London conveying 120 wagons.

The L.N.E.R. were the first Company to
reinstate Restaurant Car Service by the 9 a.m.
from Kings Cross to York on Thursday May 6th,
the third day of the strike.

Fig 64 – L. & N.E.R.'s own newspaper, 1st edition, with details on how they were coping with the strike.
(Source - Peter Hall)

Victoria and on to Marylebone, London with 3,500 churns of milk. The L. & N.E.R's newspaper trumpeted their news that the Company planned to steam 500 trains that day (compared with the L.M.S.'s 250-300) most of which would be manned by volunteers thus realising their boyhood dreams of being steam engine drivers!

Just to the south of St. Neots is a national major market gardening area running ten miles southward to Biggleswade. All produce was being shipped to London's Covent Garden Market by train from the four stations' goods yards – St. Neots, Tempsford, Sandy and Biggleswade. Covent Garden Market's business was reported as "normal". To maintain the produce's freshness and quality the Market Gardeners' Association made the decision to transport the produce by road to London three days a week.

Nationally, the T.U.C. members' response to the General Strike was patchy. Ten thousand railway workers in Crewe joined the withdrawal of labour yet a similar number at the Brunner Mond chemical works (I.C.I.) at Billingham. Co. Durham returned to their factory on Thursday. 500 railway clerks at Cardiff joined the strikers (later denied) while down the road at Newport 93% of Whitehead's steelworkers returned to their posts. Bedford Electric Works staff walked off the job but their places were taken by volunteers thus maintaining electricity generation.

The London tram network, like countless others around the country, was paralysed by a total walkout of staff but a few 'rattlers' left the depots, manned yet again by volunteers. Even the ferry links to the continent, via Dover, were stopped except for one ferry a day in each direction. This caused the Prince of Wales to take to the air and fly back to London from Paris. And so, this patchy picture was repeated the length and breadth of the country in this first week of the strike.

In the second week of the General Strike the workers seemed to be stuttering over their resolved commitment to 'see it through'. More of them were returning to work than were joining the strike. A remarkable letter was received also by the editor of the "St. Neots Advertiser" weekly newspaper which read: "Dear Sir – Many people in Nottinghamshire congratulate you and your staff in publishing the full edition of your newspaper. It was a splendid achievement and we wish you luck. From ONE OF YOUR OLDEST READERS." This coincided with the news out of the same county that the "area was devoid of excitement" suggesting the area was working normally with no reports of riots or disturbances.

All the Big Four railway companies reported the news that services were increasing to the point where they could re-start services on many branch lines. The 'Flying Scotsman' resumed running in both directions but the L. & N.E.R, could not guarantee the trains would complete their journeys. On a later day's trip, the 10th May, this illustrious express was derailed when a length of rail was removed from the permanent way at Cramlington, Northumberland by a band of 20-25 hopeful train wreckers, but no-one was injured except for a scalded volunteer fireman and a passenger's damaged ankle. The engine, no. 2565 Merry Hampton, toppled over and took five of its twelve coaches with it.

The men were, in fact, attempting to stop coal trains which were being steamed by volunteer labour. Eight were arrested eventually, and found guilty at Newcastle Assizes on July 1st. They were sentenced to between four and eight years penal servitude, but were released after between 27 and 42 months. One of the 'conspirators' was a man named William Muckle who had started work at the tender age of thirteen and received a ten pence daily wage (c.4.6p). He was an embittered young soul who carried the social injustices permeating the coal-mining industry at the time right up to his death over sixty years later.

On Saturday May 8th the L. & N.E.R. ran 750 trains, mostly using voluntary labour, 'scab' or 'blackleg' in today's parlance. Only two days later (Monday) the tally of trains puffing away was increased to 977. St. Neots Station joined in the improvements by announcing the departure of three passenger trains for London (10.30am, 12.30pm, 2.52pm) and three trains for the north (10.49am, 2.58pm and 5.48pm).

Two snippets of news that must have gripped the nation stated that the nation's tobacco allowance was one ounce per man weekly except for the Prime Minister, Stanley Baldwin, who would be able to disappear in a cloud of smoke from two ounces while relaxing in 10 Downing Street (was this an early example of parliamentary 'rule bending', as in the 2009 M.P.'s expenses scandal?).

It was also announced that the Italian airship 'Norge' had arrived in Spitsbergen to support Roald Amundsen's attempt to be the first person to fly over the North Pole. Captain Byrd arrived in Spitsbergen at the same time in a piston aircraft and, after a flight, claimed the title before Amundsen flew a day or two later. Byrd was denied the accolade weeks later after official navigational calculation checking – he missed the Pole by 80 miles so Amundsen smiled once more.

After only two weeks, the St. Neots Advertiser (Friday May 14th) trumpeted the end of this first National Strike! The return to work around the country had become a flood. It was on Wednesday May 12th the good folk of St. Neots heard on the radio that the Trades Union Congress had called off the Strike with no conditions of any sort being laid down.

There were three prominent messages heralding the termination. The first was from King George V who issued a statement which included the following: "The nation has just passed through a period of extreme anxiety. Let us not forget whatever elements of bitterness the past few days may have created, only remembering how steady and orderly the country has remained, though severely tested, and forthwith addressing ourselves to the task of bringing into being a peace which will be lasting because, forgetting the past, it looks only to the future with the hopefulness of a united people."

Prime Minister Stanley Baldwin risked re-inflaming the strife by adding: "We conceived it to be a matter of absolute duty to call upon the people to resist the menace of the general strike. The people of these islands responded to that appeal, as in our long history they have answered every claim upon their love of freedom and sense of fair play. I thank everyone."

The Chief Constable for Huntingdonshire, in which St. Neots was situated, thanked all those who had willingly offered their services as Special Constables. This voluntary act had relieved the local constabulary who had been hard-pressed due to 20 per cent of the regular force being sent to assist another police force elsewhere.

Nigel Gresley Enters the Scene and St. Neots Witnesses the Arrival of a New Generation of Express Engines

Nigel Gresley (later knighted) was appointed the last Chief Mechanical Engineer to the G.N.R. on October 1st 1911 and, after the Grouping process, Chief Mechanical Engineer of the L. & N.E.R. in February 1923. He was knighted in 1936 and died 'in post' on April 5th 1941 at the tender age of 65. He will always be immortalised in railway history by the 1930's gloriously liveried blue engine "Sir Nigel Gresley", a once regular visitor through St. Neots Station and now conserved and running steam train journeys.

In the autumn of 1922, a mere two months before the L. & N.E.R. came into existence, the chief mechanical engineers (CME) of two of the three London to Edinburgh route companies (G.N.R. and N.E.R.) were designing and building the first of a more powerful breed of locomotives called 'Pacifics', and which had a wheel arrangement known as "4-6-2". One of the first two was the iconic "Flying Scotsman".

The "Flying Scotsman" began to be constructed at Doncaster in 1922 but was not added to this new 'A1' class of goliaths until February 24th, two months after the formation of the L. & N.E.R. These engines caused a sensation with their revolutionary size and power.

The "Flying Scotsman" became famous as the first engine to run non-stop from King's Cross to Edinburgh with the help of water troughs north of York. Another record added to its curriculum vitae, is that of being the most travelled engine in the world. It was shipped to North America (1969 – organised by my old student, Nick Lord), and was the first steam engine to snort its way from Sydney to Perth in Australia.

The G.N.R., with Nigel Gresley as the new CME, was busy at the start of building a new class of Pacific locomotive called the "A1 Class", which included the "Flying Scotsman". This class was successfully introduced but needed modifications as more were built and added to the 1927 type; they were all grouped together to become known as the "A3 Class".

By 1935, Gresley wanted a new style of Pacific engine to grace the East Coast Main Line. These new streamlined boiler types were called the "A4 Pacifics", each sporting a distinctive-sounding two-tone steam whistle still heard occasionally as the conserved "Sir Nigel Gresley" steams through St. Neots pulling an excursion past ecstatic, salivating waving crowds. The first of the class was named "Silver Jubilee" to

Fig 65 – The iconic Sir Nigel Gresley. (Courtesy of Peter Hall)

Fig 66 – 'Flying Scotsman' engine speeding through St. Neots Station in the snow in the 1950s. (Joe Doncaster collection)

coincide with the celebration of the 25th year celebrations of King George V's reign in 1935.

The last Pacific engines built belonged to the Peppercorn A1 and Peppercorn A2 classes. They were designed by the L. & N.E.R. but did not enter service until 1948 which was after nationalisation of the railways. The A1 Class examples were all scrapped by British Railways; that led to the remarkable re-creation of a magnificent beast of a specimen in the form of Class A1 "Tornado", the engine built by volunteer effort in the old railway workshops in Darlington between 1990 and 2009 (see penultimate section).

"You can't get the Wood, you know!"

This subtitle was a well-worn Goon Show saying in the Fifties. The L. & N.E.R. could, however! Long before the age of 'plastic', wood was the best material for shaping into a multitude of useful commercial railway objects. Sleepers, wagons, carriages, signal-boxes, buildings; they're all there. So where did the railway companies acquire their timber apart from importing expensive quality species such as teak?

There is a village called Great Gransden about eight miles east of St. Neots which, in October 1927, had been mainly owned by the then recently deceased local squire. The village was put up for auction; houses, inns, farms, quarries and woods alike, even the windmill.

One of the woods was detailed in the auction catalogue, distinguishing between the number of hard and softwood trees. The L. & N.E.R. representative was the successful bidder, for £450, but his organisation was identified by the auctioneer as the 'Great Northern'. Old names die hard!

What would have been the uses of these different rural giants to the railway company? The tree species included:-

oak – 3,605 cubic feet

ash – 2,253 cubic feet

elm – 5,615 cubic feet

unspecified volumes and stands of Scotch pines, larch, and hornbeam.

Once felled, the trunks were dressed and transported to St. Neots Station for dispatch to the company's workshops, the hardwoods for carriage and wagon frames while the softwoods would be for sleepers, wagon planks and general building materials.

Tempsford Station comes under the 'wing' of St. Neots Station

Tempsford Station officially opened for business on January 1st 1863, nearly thirteen years after the grand opening ceremony of the line. The day-to-day running of its operation was independent, within the company, until 1931 after which it came under the management wing of the St. Neots stationmaster. This may have been in response to the dark days of the Great Depression, downturn in trade and required economies.

During World War Two, the station regained its independent status in 1942 with the appointment of a Mr. Archer as stationmaster when a more senior figure

Fig 67 – King George VI, behind Queen Elizabeth on Tempsford Station in November 1943, arriving from Huntingdon to inspect Tempsford Hall after decorating the 'Heroes of Telemark' at Gaynes Hall, Grafham Water. Stationmaster Archer is in the background nearest the carriage.

(Courtesy of Peter Hall)

was essential on the 'doorstep' of Tempsford Hall (now the head office of Kier's, builders). The Hall had become the main spy training centre for the U.K. with its adjacent airfield being the take-off point for agents departing for enemy territory by parachute. Although the most famous agents travelled to and fro by car, the Government needed someone on the spot to monitor passengers using the station. After all, there were German spies in the area!

The station's most auspicious day was on November 9th 1943 when King George V1 and Queen Elizabeth (the late Queen Mother) visited Gaynes Hall ('Station 61'), a mere seven miles from St. Neots and adjacent to Grafham Water. The occasion was to decorate the remaining Norwegian Heroes of Telemark and British saboteurs, all of whom having been secretly brought in by the 'Shetland Bus' days beforehand.

They attempted to stop Hitler from building the first atom bomb but only temporarily wrecked the Rjukan Vemork power plant for three months before it was rebuilt to continue the production of 'heavy water' (deuterium). The final load of deuterium was destroyed as it was ferried across a lake between railheads (by Kirk Douglas in the drama film of the same name) in the winter of 1944. Had they failed, you most probably would not have been reading this book.

The King and Queen then returned to Huntingdon and on to Tempsford Station, via St. Neots, to inspect Tempsford Hall, two and a half miles further on. I am aware of the details of the story from my Norwegian friend whose father was one of the Heroes but chose to stay behind to support Max Manus, the leader of the Norwegian Underground saboteurs.

Fig 68 – Tempsford Station, from Station Road, 1950. (Joe Doncaster Collection)

After the War, Tempsford reverted to coming under the wing of Mr. Archer who, by 1945, was in charge of St. Neots Station. He lived in Eynesbury in his own house, and found it convenient to splutter down the A1 on his motorcycle to Tempsford on inspection forays at regular intervals until the station closed on November 5th 1956.

Ken Barringer's Interview with Joe Doncaster, Station employee for 40 years

Transcribed from the cassette (taped c.1970) with additional research in italics by the author.

Joe Doncaster was born in late-1906 at Cambridge Street, St. Neots. His father was a domestic coachman who was born in March, Cambridgeshire. Joe was a pupil at Huntingdon Grammar School in World War One. When he left school, he joined either the G.N.R or the L. & N.E.R. By 1930 he was at Biggleswade, Bedfordshire before being transferred to Huntingdon North Station as a goods clerk in November 1930.

Joe was only there until July the following year before he came to St. Neots, eventually

rising to become senior Goods Agent at an unknown date. He retired in the mid-1960s. Although he never married he had a girlfriend, and lived with his widowed mother in the middle house of a 3-unit terraced block immediately to the east of the Total petrol station on Cambridge Street (in Green End).

A tall, slim gentleman and tennis player, Joe was an avid amateur photographer who 'snapped' many unusual and special engines as they passed through St. Neots on the ECML. His office was in the goods warehouse opposite the North Signal-box. The signalman would forewarn Joe of an impending 'interesting' train and the latter would be ready with his camera. Joe often entered his photographs in competitions in Birmingham and St. Neots, winning occasional prizes.

"You asked me to tape some memories. Of course, there are some memories we shall never forget, particularly the nights when St. Neots was bombed during the war.

I woke in the early hours and the house was shaking like mad so I decided it was time to get up. I waited with my mother (who had a glass of whisky to steady her nerves) until morning when I decided to go down to Shortsands to have a look round.

There was a trail of incendiaries from the railway right the way across what used to be Smith's Big Field, and some narrowly missed the football stand (at the old St. Neots FC football pitch behind the Bull's Head pub in Cambridge St.).

On the same night, September 27th 1940, they dropped two small bombs near the houses in Mill Lane (at the end of The Common) and two bombs in the garden of the (now demolished) Engine & Tender pub (opposite the north end of Cromwell Road). The biggest bomb of all was dropped in what was Wittamore's Field near the football ground and St. Mary's School at the end of Wintringham Road. That was a real shaker. I picked up an incendiary bomb that hadn't gone off and walked to the gate of Shortsands and gave it to Sergeant Musby. The total number of devices dropped on that night was 20 high explosive and 50 incendiary bombs; the Germans were probably after disrupting the railway line.

The 'Thunderbolt' incident occurred at 5pm. Phyllis Harvey had finished (her shift at the railway station where she worked) and she came to me to ask if I'd look up some train times for her. There was a terrific roar outside and the noise of an aircraft and, being interested in aircraft, I went to have a look. Looking towards Abbotsley I saw a Thunderbolt spinning down without a tail and the pilot parachuting safely down to land at Tithe Farm. The plane landed in a field between Lower Wintringham and the railway line. I went up there next morning but everything had been cleared away by then.

The roar we heard was the aircraft that flew over the town and crashed in a field near St. Neots Golf Club. They didn't find the remains until developers got a bulldozer on the job when they started to build the new houses (Milton Avenue Estate off Crosshall Road – 1969). I think the engine was taken to Bassingbourn, where I used to visit as a volunteer (did Joe mean Duxford?).

I remember seeing a Dornier when I was having breakfast one morning. It was flying due west and must have been the one that bombed Bedford Station.

On another occasion I was in the Station Porters' Room at 12 0'clock just before I went home and there was one lone Spitfire flying due south. Directly after that the air raid siren sounded. Shortly after that I had to go down town and, on the way back, I was outside Freeman, Hardy & Willis's shoe shop (opposite Barretts store) when the all-clear sounded. I went home to have my dinner when I heard all these aircraft dashing about and there were these three Hurricanes; I didn't see the Germans. I looked over towards Abbotsley again and I saw like three silver stars careering about. Soon after that you heard the machine guns going, and that was the one they brought down behind the "Bell" pub at Eaton Socon (now site of Kentucky Fried Chicken Drive-thru, adjacent to B & Q).

I remember the one that bombed Little Barford Power Station (the old coal-fired one). I think that, if the fighters had left him alone he wouldn't have dropped his bombs. That was the incident where the main power house was strafed leaving bullet marks and bomb damaged bricks; a workman picked up an unexploded bomb and dropped it in the river!. I was at home then and I saw 'Nate' Ashwell diving about from one side of the goods warehouse to the other. 'Nate' shouted he thought it was a German. The aircraft banked over the allotments at the back of our house, about where Charles Street is now, and I saw these black crosses on the side. I think that was the aircraft that shot up one of our engine tenders the other side of Priory Hill Bridge.

On one Sunday morning I was going to work at 9 o'clock and counted 108 Liberators going out on a bombing raid. Another regular sight was the Flying Fortresses. They'd go round and round starting with nine. They'd be joined by 9 more – still all going round. Eighteen then 27, 36, 45 and so on. The sun was shining on them, with silver paint in those days. Later in the day, looking towards Cambridge, you'd see these unfortunate devils come limping back with some engines not working and shot about wholesale. You knew there would be some casualties there. This was all tied up with another job I didn't like to see but it was all to do with war. A few days after, you'd see a lorry load of little green boxes no bigger than a cigar or shoe box full of belongings of those poor devils who had been killed. We had the job of sending them to Liverpool for shipment back to America.

Talking of the Americans, their transport officer, Louis Galway, used to spend a lot of time in this office; a jolly nice boy. He used to come up here in a jeep, and one day he knocked a young tree over next to the weighbridge. He used to use carbon paper only once before stacking it and giving it to me. I got loads of the stuff. He kept me supplied with tobacco, too.

The American officers and nurses used to step off the trains, usually the 5.47pm, commandeer my office and get on to Diddington Hospital (a huge hospital in the fields surrounding Diddington Church, one mile south of Buckden adjacent to the A1 road) for transport. They were a snobbish lot; they'd never speak to you. There was always a nasty, musty smell in the office after the nurses had been in. I suppose it was their particular disinfectant they used.

Sometimes, if it was foggy and you looked over Graveley way, you'd see "FIDO" working. That was the 'Fog Dispersal' system where they burnt paraffin alongside the runway for take-off and landing safely.

Also stationed at Graveley at that time was a Flight Lieutenant McDonald, a Canadian pilot who used to fly Halifaxes. He used to come to our ATC (Air Training Corps) model aeroplane club meetings. He took one of my models on a raid to Dusseldorf. It was the night after the 1,000 bomber raid and it came back the worse for wear. Unfortunately, I lost it when I moved house.

Another party I used to get through the station was of Resistance troops. You'd have about a dozen of them get off the 5.55pm train. They were all in different uniforms. They'd get picked up and taken to Gaynes Hall and, after a course of training, they would get taken to Tempsford Airfield to fly out and be dropped by parachute. If they 'chickened out' they used to bring them back and lock them up because they knew too much, so they daren't let them out loose (what really happened to these men during and at the end of the War is not known, but rumours have begun to surface and they will be investigated).

Also at Gaynes Hall, they used to have what they called FANYS, or Field Ambulance Nursing Yeomanry. They were real ladies, not common-or-garden ATS for that job. Some of them were titled ladies, too. They were about as forthcoming as the Yanks when they were in the office.

I was in that office for about 13 years. I knew everyone at that time, and everybody knew me. Of course, the population was very different from what it is today. One of my regulars used to be Lord Eltisley (from Croxton Hall). He would come for his first class ticket to London and ask first: "Can I offer you a cigarette?" Out came a gold cigarette case and through the window would come two Dunhill Turkish cigarettes.

Dick Rowley would often go up to London for a night. Two darned great leather suitcases. He always emptied his purse out at the booking office window to pay you. Talking of the Rowleys, the chap had a little box of fish from Boston every night. Years ago, Tim somebody, who used to live down the borough (St. Neots town) used to fetch it, and sometimes Ben Freestone fetched it. When the Rowley boys were home, George and John would fetch it. John was always a perfect little gentleman but unfortunately he went shell-shocked. I suppose he's still at St. Andrew's Nursing Home, poor boy. A real little gentleman, he was.

Then over at Gt. Staughton, we had the Duberly's, the Grays, and the Comptons. I remember old Gray had a nipped-in trilby. Compton's nose was purple. Young Gray, he was a naval officer, married Gray-Duberly. She was a very pretty girl and, years before, she was presented at Court.

It was only a year or two ago I was coming down the back stairs when young Gray spotted me. He asked me how I was; he was a thorough gentleman was young Gray. Then there was the Honorable Mrs. Duberly. I believe, years ago, she used to live at Gaynes Hall.

I remember one night she came into the booking office and she wanted to use the telephone. She was smoking one of those horrid Turkish cigarettes. She said, "You must have one of my oatmeal biscuits." There was I eating her oatmeal biscuits and she was smoking Turkish cigarettes. It was bloody horrible when she'd gone. A lot of these people used to come into the office in winter just to warm themselves in front of my fire. It didn't matter about me!

Then there was Alfie Hine, traveller for Jordan & Addington. He used to go up to Peterborough, Spalding and Stamford markets for corn. His mate, Charlie Jones, used to go up to London a lot.

Paine & Co.'s representatives were Walter Nicholls (he had a gruff voice), Jackie Scott and Arthur Middleton. Arthur used to go up to the Station Hotel for his walk every Sunday morning. He was secretary of Paine & Co. and he was registered for the Station Hotel. We thought he used to take that walk just to keep an eye on that place for Paine & Co. Quite probable, and have a pint in the process!

Still with Paine & Co., their coal used to come into the goods yard and was carted down town by two horses and carts. One little boy with a club foot called Barringer – don't know whether he was related to you or not – and Paul Smith, Noel Smith's father. Mr. Gaunt, who lived at Shortsands Cottage, used to cart a lot of their grain with a cart and trolley.

The Paper Mill, Little Paxton Bridge place, used to have two steam lorries. Jack Hagan on the old Sentinel and Tony Ashman drove the Burrell. They used to take the coal back and collect the paper. I used to find the steam engines very useful because I could put my smoking pipes on one of the steam pipes and they were clear of 'gunge' when they'd finished with them.

Another important customer was Colonel

Pank who used to live on the corner of Bushmead Road in Eaton Socon. (He was appointed aide-de-camp to King George VI in 1929, which possibly explained his influence over the following tale). I always remember the first time I saw him. Apparently, people had been trying to get the 5 o'clock train out of King's Cross to stop at St. Neots, but with no success. He came into the office one day and said: "The 5 o'clock doesn't stop here, does it?" I said: "No, but a lot of people have tried to get it stopped but they won't do anything about it." He said: "Well, the directors have promised me it'll stop on the next timetable." I thought "Blimey, I've got to look after you, mate." Sure enough, next timetable it stopped!

He was a thorough gentleman, although he was old Middlesex Regiment (a.k.a. Duke of Cambridge's Own, 1755-1966). Paul Ashwell, stationmaster, was Duke of Cornwall's Light Infantry (1702-1959) and they used to go one against the other, and Paul Ashwell made sure he knew more about firearms than 'tanker' did. They didn't have much to say to one another after that (this rivalry and animosity must have been associated with the 1st World War involvement of both regiments) .

Then there was Mr. Hodge of Paxton Hall. Mr. Hodge was a tall man, well over 6 feet (just short of 2 metres) and he used to drive a tiny Triumph, like a baby Austin without a hood. His youngest daughter married Jack Rycroft, the builder.

In those days, J.R. Smith used to send away a lot of pork pies after making them at the back of the station buildings. Nothing unusual in that except he started to send one pound (0.5 kgm.) in a brown paper parcel to a Mrs. Robinson of Glasswell, Aberdeenshire every now and then. The

Fig 69 – Foden Sentinel steam lorry belonging to Jordan & Addington that delivered to and from the station warehouse to the brewery and around the town in the 1920-1930s.

(Courtesy of Judith Addington)

carriage was 7d (3p), which I think was the smallest rate we ever charged.

After the war, the Kimbolton Grammar School cadets were going away for their annual camp. All the stuff loaded up in tea chests, boxes and so on. We were eager to get it loaded up and on to the platform. We had one of those 4-wheeled barrows with "Master" painted on. With no lift for the footbridge we had to lift the barrow over the rails. It got to a point where one wheel was stuck over a rail. Of course, there happened to be a train coming, and there was one almighty bang. Thereafter, for 400 yards, there were papers strewn all along the track to Rowley's Priory Hill Bridge to the north. It just suited the boys. I've never seen such a mess in my life. It could have been worse.

When Jim Sawford worked at the Cross Keys he used to come up to the station in their bus regularly to meet the trains. I remember a chap called Kightley, he died a little while back, and he stood leaning over the ironwork there. He was 'miles away'. Jim crept up behind him and shouted "You didn't catch me." Poor old Jim nearly fell off the steps.

Fig 70 – Gresley designed Class A4 "Dominion of Canada" (Courtesy of Peter Hall)

Jim told me another story, where he was working for Bull's the builders. He took a load of gravel to the Wilbrahams at Paxton Hill House. He was driving up and down and couldn't find anyone to tell him what to do. He met this tall bloke walking along the road and said to him "I say, mate. Do you think the old Major'll mind if I drop this load down here? The man said: "I am the Major." Collapse of poor Jim.

Talking of the Wilbrahams, there was Mrs. Wilbraham, a tall stately lady with smartly groomed hair. She was a frequent visitor. She used to breed Angora rabbits and she was a show judge. She used to send the Angora wool up to Yorkshire from time to time for processing. But she was never very friendly.

Going back further still, I'll never forget the trial run of the A4 "Silver Jubilee" engine. I've never seen a train go through St. Neots like it. But a little later they had to stop and drop one of the coaches off in the 'up' siding. I thought I'd try it for comfort. Those First Class seats were no softer than the other Third Class seats. I was quite disappointed with it.

Then on another occasion, the A4 "Dominion of Canada" was put off here in the sidings broken down; a fine blue engine. I got up on the footplate. There were dirty old bricks and mortar there. It took the glamour out of steam engines to see them like that. You've never seen such a filthy sight. You'd got the real thing then.

Another character you used to see up at the station was Charlie the shunt horse. He really hated trains. Eric used to hitch Charlie to a rail in the goods yard when the horse wasn't working, but he always tried to pull away from the track when a train passed by. When Eric had finished duty he'd unhitch Charlie and let him find his own way back to the stable in the Station Hotel yard about 100 yards away.

Charlie would always stand patiently outside the hotel porch. If he didn't get any attention there, he'd go and tap his head on the bar-room window. Eventually, Eric would come out with a drink of beer for him.

I was up there the evening the goods warehouse and granary burnt down in 1968. I was down near the booking office when there was an almighty bang. I flew to the goods office. The explosion had made an awful mess of things………."

(End of tape)

The interview ends abruptly at this point, but it preserves for posterity the way of life of a mid-Twentieth Century market town's involvement with its main means of transport and connection with the outside world. It gives you a vivid picture of St. Neots Station life during the middle of the last century and the World's greatest conflict. Compare that with today's technological advances and demands for speed in communication, delivery, action, service and many other aspects of modern life that are dominated by computers and digitalisation. The following photographs were taken by Joe Doncaster.

Chapter Five

World War Two, Nationalisation & Electrification

Wartime Railway Executive Structure and Advertisements on Railway Usage

During the World War Two period, advertisements appeared at regular intervals related to the railways' support for the War effort. A sample of them appears at this point to savour the flavour of those times. It will be noticed that the four great companies were combined into one unitary system, a prelude to the accession to power of the Labour Party in the 1945 general election, and the nationalisation of the whole U.K. railway network on January 1st 1948. How, and when, did the former event occur?

The United Kingdom declared war on Germany on Sunday September 3rd 1939 and, as part of the preparations for this momentous decision, it was announced in the press on the previous day that, as from midnight September 2nd, all Britain's

In the BLACK-OUT

The Railways are giving as much light as they are permitted. You can make the black-out " lighter " if you—

- Keep the blinds down.
- Tell your fellow passengers the names of the stations.
- Be sure your train is at the platform before alighting.
- Close the carriage door after you.
- Have your ticket ready at the barrier.

RAILWAY EXECUTIVE COMMITTEE

RAIL TRANSPORT
is "Half the Battle"

A MILLION LOADED WAGONS are hauled by the Railways every week

BRITISH RAILWAYS
GWR · LMS   LNER · SR
CARRY THE WAR LOAD

Blue Prints are ready

The post-war schemes on the Main Line Railways include plans for tracks capable of running speeds of at least 80 miles an hour; the reconstruction of bridges; widening of lines; the completion of electrification works stopped by the war and, later, the rebuilding of hundreds of stations on the most modern lines.

In the meantime the railways are working 24 hours a day to carry the supplies needed for victory.

GWR · LMS · LNER · SR

Fig 71 – A selection of railway World War Two advertisements issued by the wartime Railway Executive. (Source – author)

railways passed under Government control. This was done by an order made by the Minister of Transport, who appointed a six-man Railway Executive Committee to act on his behalf. The six were:-

Sir Ralph Wedgwood, 'recently' retired from the general managership of the L.&N.E.R.; C.H. Newton, general manager of the L.&N.E.R.; Frank Pick, vice-chairman of London Passenger Transport Board; Sir James Milne, general manager of S.R.; and Sir William Wood, vice-president of L.M.S. Sir Ralph was to be chairman of the new Committee, which was to be in charge of all the main line railways, the London passenger network (including the Underground) and five small local lines.

Finally, with the war's end and a Labour Party in power, the "Big 4" attempted to reclaim ownership. Nationalisation occurred on January 1st 1948, a giant political step following the nationalisation of the private health structure of the country.

The Demise of the Station's Goods Yards

There was a multitude of reasons why the goods facilities were withdrawn from the Station, a process which was mirrored all around the country. Road haulage began to grow soon after the dawn of the Twentieth Century. The manufacture of lorries for the First World War was so great that, by its cessation, Army sales flooded the towns and cities with lorries, and unemployed men were only too eager to jump at this new job opportunity.

According to Gilbert Walker and Professor Colin Divall (Railway Studies Dept., York University), this mass of small operators was committed to intense price competition from the start, in order to get a 'foot in the door'; this quickly transformed the situation. Service quality was also often thought to be better, with more rapid transit, less pilferage and fewer breakages among the advantages being widely cited.

By 1921, estimates of the loss of rail freight to hauliers was some six million tons annually. The following year saw the railway companies failing to gain statutory powers to operate road haulage independently of their railway operations. Although they finally succeeded in 1928, this delay further blunted the railways' competitive edge and forced them to continue short-haul goods services which some wanted to abandon. By 1935, over half of the railways' traffic in general merchandise had been lost to road.

World War Two repeated the same lorry and manpower surplus. Railways' goods trade shrinkage began in earnest after the highly mobile Second World War when all the unwanted equipment was auctioned to all and sundry.

One aspect of traffic to be hit at St. Neots was market gardening. The Cretaceous Greensand escarpment, which crossed the River Ivel valley about seven to nine miles to the south at the appropriately named town of Sandy, was severely denuded by melt-water at the end of the Ice Age. The sand was washed down the Ivel and Great Ouse valleys to create a huge skim of sandy soil which was exploited by farmers.

Farmers, realising that the sandy base, as opposed to wetter thicker clays elsewhere, warmed up quicker by a fortnight's margin in springtime. By using the adjacent railway stations of Biggleswade, Sandy, Tempsford and St. Neots, the farmers were able to capture the earlier higher prices in London and compete effectively against most other regions.

Throughout most of the year the station areas tended to be dominated by the distinctive whiffs of a wide range of vegetables; carrots, spring and pickling onions, radishes, lettuces, cauliflowers, cabbages, potatoes, Brussels' sprouts and cut flowers, all of which were affectionately handled with care.

At the end of the European sector of the War, on May 8th 1945, a huge amount of army surplus vehicles was auctioned off. Local entrepreneurial types bought the lorries and began to pinch the railway transport contracts. Once the lorries had been loaded they were off down the fifty miles of the Great North Road to Covent Garden and back home again by late lunchtime. It eliminated the double trans-

shipment costs and fear of produce damage of rail. And the food was so much the fresher. The railway's trade evaporated quickly. One such local transport company, H. E. Payne of Wyboston, grew from strength to strength and their traffic is a common sight on the London road today.

The goods yards closed in stages, between 1960 and 1983, as the trade was lost to road competition. Two of its landmark post-war contracts included the shipment of huge concrete beams, for bridge construction on the 1959 M1 Motorway, from the adjacent Booth Concrete factory on Station Road. One of the last jobs, in 1965, was to receive the massive concrete rings for the water conduits being installed at Grafham Reservoir six miles up the A1 trunk-road and adjacent to Gaynes Hall.

Fig 72 – A cauliflower 6-plank wagon no. 401648 (ex-GNR 1648). Chassis plate reads: "To be returned to St Neots". It is fitted with upper rails for vegetable traffic and in LNER livery Nov. 1926. (Courtesy of Peter Hall)

Fig 73 – The last steam goods engine to serve St. Neots goods yards. (Joe Doncaster Collection)

A Bombshell; St. Neots Station is Likely to Close

The date was Monday October 24th 1961. The experience of World War One's Government takeover of the railway companies under the umbrella of the 'Railway Executive', which led to the 1923 Grouping of Companies into the 'Big Four', triggered a similar scheme during the Second World War to be followed by nationalisation in 1948.

Despite the leadership qualities of Winston Churchill during the War, the nation chose Clement Atlee to lead a socialist government a few months after the cessation of hostilities in August 1945. Nationalisation proceeded to the end of the decade to include coalmines, road transport, health industry and railways.

January 1st 1948 dawned to see the nation's ownership of St. Neots Station! This meant that decisions on the station's operations, and its destiny, were finalised in London's committee rooms, now highly influenced by government policy.

St. Neots had lost its wartime airfield importance (six in the vicinity), industry had stagnated and its population had shrunk back into a typical market town pattern. Road transport was gnawing away at the volume of rail goods traffic using the station, and private car rationing ceased in 1954. All this combined to erode the station's importance to the town's daily life; passenger patronage was less than one hundred a day.

The new Railway Executive evolved to become known as the 'British Railways' by 1961 when the local traffic manager, Mr. G. F. Huskisson, chaired a press conference at Hitchin on October 24th 1961. In the hindsight of the intervening years, to today, cynics among readers could be forgiven for thinking that Mr. Huskisson's introductory statement was pure political 'spin'. The chairman said he had "improvements to services and the introduction of cheaper day excursion fares to announce, all of which would operate from November 6th". The new passenger timetable was, at this point, "experimental".

A St. Neots reporter questioned Mr. Huskisson by telling him frankly that the proposals were not "improvements" but a definite 'thumbs down' for St. Neots. The reporter said that the town was to lose its Sunday excursion to London for the first (peace) time in decades.

This acidification of the atmosphere in the room must have unsettled Mr. Huskisson because he had a far greater bombshell to burst over the assembly. He proceeded by stating that, due to the drop in passenger patronage at St. Neots, there was a "very real possibility" the station would close to passengers. But the goods yard was under no threat whatsoever.

When asked for details, Mr. Huskisson said that Huntingdon, Biggleswade and Sandy stations were safe from closure. Huntingdon's served the county town and the still-important handful of nearby air bases, Biggleswade's was just that bit nearer London for commuters, and Sandy's was a rail junction with its Oxford, Bedford and Cambridge cross-country route. Offord and Tempsford stations had already closed in 1956.

Fair comment, use it or lose it, but Mr. Huskisson's comments were based on retrospective facts. No thought had been given to any future developments until the

St. Neots reporter generated debate. The traffic manager asked the reporter if there were any St. Neots developments in the offing.

Mr. Huskisson should have been discussing that topic with the town's Council whereupon he would have discovered that the London Overspill programme was about to sprout before the end of the year thus leading to, at least, an eventual trebling of the population! It was to be a further 18 months before the infamous Dr. Beeching's Report on the future of Britain's railways was to be published. This is a typical example of the sort of unsystematic thinking that plagued officialdom half a century ago.

A lengthy discussion ensued during which Mr. Huskisson 'leaked' the news that the anticipated announcement for the route's electrification date was to be deferred for at least an enormous seven years. In fact, the reporters were told categorically that it could be discounted. There were logistical problems at Hitchin, Welwyn Viaduct and insufficient room for terminating trains at King's Cross. Further problems, created by lack of money for track widening schemes at Arlesey, Sandy, Huntingdon, and Holme to Yaxley, compounded the situation.

In reality, electrified services did not occur until 1987, twenty six years later! Lack of finance placed these planned schemes in abeyance. The meeting broke up acrimoniously with the 'Sword of Damocles' hanging over St. Neots station's future for another eighteen months at which point the infamous Dr. Beeching appeared on the national scene.

At the end of March 1963 Dr. Beeching presented his Report on what he thought should happen to the British passenger and goods railway network. He had been appointed by the MacMillan government to "sort out the railways" and make them profitable. That last word is laughable when one compares the enormous £140 million deficit of 1962 and the current State borrowing level of today (2009).

True, the railways were suffering very badly from road and air transport competition but, when one studies the maps detailing what was ripped up and the demands of the past decade, no wonder the various authorities and pressure groups are tearing their hair out in frustration. Stations are being re-opened, and lines have been ear-marked for rebuilding in a July 2009 government report. But, who knows where the money is going to appear from?

On a local scale, and when the Nineteenth Century railway expansion had concluded, even small towns and villages often boasted a railway station. Ramsey had two stations and St. Ives proudly advertised five routes sprouting from the town centre starfish-like. It is now all ripped apart. Some of the old tracks have become roads such as the St. Ives, Needingworth and Chatteris bypasses. Other lines were re-digested into farmland while some have become nature walk wonderlands, carefully nurtured by councils and support groups.

Dr. Beeching's infamous Report stated that all stations would remain "under review" where viability was concerned. Almost immediately the Report was published Mr. Huskisson re-appeared, uttering stern words to say that St. Neots, Sandy and Biggleswade stations had been "financially suspect for years". He really was trying to put the knife in! The Damoclese sword thread stretched a little narrower overnight! The scepticism vented at the 1961 press conference, regarding the 'Huskisson wriggling' over a

new timetable to attract new patrons, was well-founded because yet another batch of 'new services' was announced.

Distinctive Sounds Arrive at St. Neots Station

At the end of the 1950s, a new engine roared through the station. The last steam engine, 'Evening Star', had rolled out of the workshops in 1959. At about the same time, a new type of diesel-electric engine was being developed and trials occurred along the main line. Its unique piston arrangement created a distinctive sound that would thrill 'anoraks and gricers' for the next two decades. Even my own son had such a powerful dream about "Ballymoss", one of these thoroughbreds, he sat bolt upright in bed and screamed the place down he had seen the engine – but remembered nothing of this episode next morning! He never did see it.

The name of this type? The famous 'Deltic' prototype, with its distinctive seagull motif proudly displayed on each end, appeared around 1959 and graced the East Coast Main Line for the next two years (now preserved by the National Railway Museum annexe at Shildon Railway Museum, Co. Durham). At the time, this new class was the most powerful diesel engine in the world. Its engine was tweaked and modified, and eventually 22 of the class, to be named after famous racehorses and British Army regiments, came into service through St. Neots during 1961 and 1962. They were so economical, they replaced 55 Pacific steam engines.

The Deltics began to show their age by the mid-1970s. Their power, and the work that was squeezed out of them, began to show

Fig 74 – Final prototype version of Co-Co English Electric Type 5 named 'Deltic' (no. 1) heading for King's Cross in winter c.1959 with iconic gull-wing motif on the front. The engine is now preserved at Shildon Railway Museum, Co. Durham (annexe of NRM, York). At the time, it was the most powerful diesel engine in Europe; built by English Electric, Preston. Only 21 were built for use on the East Coast Main Line from 1961-81. They were powered by two Napier 'Deltic' 18-cylinder engines contributing to a total engine weight of 99 tons.

(Joe Doncaster Collection)

Signal Boxes

There were two signal boxes at St. Neots, North and South. They were designed to oversee the operations of the two goods yards as well as police the main line traffic. They were operated manually using lever frames, muscle and, probably, plenty of spinach sandwiches for the signalman's lunch.

The two boxes were built in 1877 but, when the line was quadrupled in 1898, the South box was rebuilt to match the wooden North box architecturally. The North box was sited at the side of the London-bound slow 'up' line about 100 metres north of the platforms while the South box was situated in a similar easterly position a few metres north of the Cambridge Road bridge; its brick foundations can still be seen on the embankment side.

signs of metal fatigue in their bodywork. They began to be replaced by the high speed trains, the HST 125s, and from 1975 they were gradually relegated to local services between King's Cross and Peterborough. The engine sound of a Deltic starting from allowing passengers to disembark at St. Neots, turned railway patrons' heads for a further six years.

The advent of HST 125s, travelling at 125 mph and introduced in 1975, caused the railway authorities to paint restricted access lines on platforms to protect waiting passengers from being sucked into the carriages as they passed by. The engines had motive power units at both ends thus solving the problem of metal fatigue, but not one was scheduled to stop at St. Neots at any time thus condemning travellers to the then two-car diesel 25-year old design conceived when the Ford Prefect was fashionable.

Fig 75 – South Signal box, St. Neots, 1978, with a somewhat despondent signalman, Bert Thaxter, after his last shift. The North signal box can be seen in Fig. 47 in 1895.

(Courtesy of St. Neots Museum)

The North box was decommissioned and removed in 1925 after the L. & N.E.R. removed many signal boxes to save money. Complete control of the station layout and main line operation was concentrated at the South box. Dramatic innovations in signalling saw all local signal boxes become unnecessary, so the South box ceased functioning on December 10th 1977. Monitoring of the main line was accomplished from the new state-of-the-art Everton Crossing main box (north of Sandy) thereafter, and signals became automated by the trains themselves.

The Last Working Steam Engine in St. Neots

St. Neots had one more surprise to 'tickle the delights' of the area's railway enthusiasts. You could be forgiven for thinking that the last working steam engine to grace the silver rails of the local lines was on the main line. Forget it!

At the south end of St. Neots, a shade over one mile from the station, stands a modern gas-fired electricity power station. It opened about 1995, replacing an earlier coal-fired power station and sited next to the river for cooling water. It was opened around 1930, its 65 metre chimney and two cooling towers dominating the surrounding landscape so much that the German bomber pilots used it as a navigational beacon to provide them with greater accuracy directing them to their various city targets.

The new power station receives its natural gas via a pipeline, but the earlier coal-fired station was fed by trainloads of coal either being delivered from the New England, Peterborough marshalling yard or from the Bedford St. John's to Sandy North Junction line where a special wartime double-line curve was installed in 1940 to allow an alternative coal supplies' route to access the power station for if the main line was bombed, as indeed it was at St. Neots; even the power station itself was attacked. The curve was removed in 1962.

The Peterborough supply trains had to travel down to Tempsford to gain access to the correct line leading to the power station's sidings but, as the line leading a few hundred metres to the power station was of insufficient strength to support mainline engines, the power station proudly owned its very own shunting steam engine which operated until 1978, ten years after the last British Railways scheduled mainline steam-hauled service. The engine was replaced by a small diesel shunter.

What was this gem of a miraculous survivor? It was a small blue-painted tank engine built by Andrew Barclay, Sons & Co. Ltd. at Kilmarnock in 1939 as unit no. 2069. It had 14" x 22" cylinders and 3' 5" wheels for the 'anoraks' lurking amongst readers, and was named "Little Barford". After 24 years service there it was transferred to Goldington Power Station, Bedford in November 1963 and then on to Acton Lane Power Station in London in July 1965. From there it travelled to the Foxfield Railway in Staffordshire for preservation in March 1981. After a 'spit and polish' job, it proceeded to the Manchester Science & Industry Museum in 1995 until its final resting place at the Mid Suffolk Light Railway where this little nomad delights summertime pulling intrepid travellers through the undulating county's countryside.

The engine was replaced at Little Barford by another Barclay's steam engine which continued to work, albeit intermittently,

Fig 76 – 'Little Barford' in steam at Little Barford Power Station, St. Neots in 1960. (George Pring Collection)

until 1982 when it was replaced finally by a small diesel shunter.

Electrification, at last! No more Changing at Hitchin for King's Cross

After all the hopes, aspirations and tantalizing promises of yesteryear, British Rail announced, in 1980, that electrification of the East Coast Main Line would commence within three years.

Contractors sank the first bases for the overhead gantries at King's Cross in January 1981 coupled with assurances from British Rail that "electrification will arrive in the shortest possible time". That phrase was full of potential mousetraps of delay. By the November there were depressing comments from St. Neots Council and the Railway Development Society may well force the

closure of the town station because of the dilapidated unreliability of the two-car diesel units conceived (passengers had been promised 90 mph double glazed trains with all mod-cons). These comments were repudiated immediately by British Rail's Divisional Manager Bill Parker.

Electrification would mean new work practices for the train crews with the introduction of flexible rosters and a new productivity agreement. The proposals upset the ASLEF union (Associated Society of Locomotive Engineers & Firemen). John Major, M.P. for Huntingdon and Parliamentary Private Secretary, knew how poor the local service was to London; he lived in Great Stukeley, just north-west of Huntingdon. He experienced the journey that could take ninety minutes with a train change at Hitchin at the half way stage.

On January 3rd 1983 John Major was "hopeful the ASLEF dispute will be settled shortly" and, once that occurred, he would oversee British Rail's formal application for the money to install the full infrastructure to Edinburgh. His comments were successful and, by January 1984 the concrete bases had been sunk through St. Neots Station and on northwards. The plan was for the full scheme to be up-and-running by early 1990 with new streamlined trains.

Fig 77 – View of St. Neots Station approach from the north in 1983 showing the old North Goods Yard access siding and the recently installed concrete bases for the electric wire-support masts prior to the electrification of the line.
(Source – St. Neots Advertiser)

The use of 25,000-volts overhead wires meant that all the relevant bridges had to be replaced to accommodate the wires, especially Skew Bridge one mile north of St. Neots Station. The skew design, pioneered by George Stephenson on his famous Stockton & Darlington Railway over the River Gaunless, Co. Durham in 1825, was used in 1898 when the line was quadrupled. Paxton Bridge had carried millions of vehicles during nearly a century of usage but it had to go.

The first job was to build a temporary Bailey bridge to maintain the flow of traffic. Then, on Sunday November 20th 1983,

old wooden sleepers were placed to protect the lines when explosives attempted to demolish the bridge. The men huffed and puffed but the bridge would not fall down; insufficient explosives had been implanted showing the bridge had been built to last. Even the second larger 'dose' did not fully complete the task, so a machine had to be brought in to complete the job.

Once the new concrete bridge had been constructed the overhead wires were duly installed; the scene at the station took on a more cluttered appearance. The new electric service arrived at the beginning of January 1987 with the appearance of the new Class 90 electric express trains at speeds of up to 140 mph, none being scheduled to stop. The old local two-car diesels were gracefully retired, and replaced by the current four-car electric units. Even more important was the new working timetable which extended their route from Huntingdon to Peterborough in the north and eliminated the train change at Hitchin altogether with through running to King's Cross. In addition, trains ran every half hour, guaranteed four carriages and running speeds of up to 90 mph thus chopping many minutes of travelling time to and from London.

This was music to the ears, and commuter numbers swelled the platforms during the rush hours. Now came the need for extra car parking, and the old North Goods Yard was cleared of a few rusting old tracks and coal merchant's stockpiles. The car park was surfaced, lighting, and security cameras installed. The old image of the station buzzing with the activity of a market town and its associated agricultural processing industries now took on the role of commuter station supporting the expanding housing estates built in the town; the population has now

Fig 78 – The two stages in the demolition of 'Skew Bridge', Paxton Hill, St. Neots, 1983. The first photo shows an HST125 diesel passing the site.
(Source – 'St. Neots Advertiser')

doubled, from fifteen to thirty thousand, since 1975 to 2010.

Nationalised British Railways 1948-1996 and Privatisation

After nationalisation, all the standard gauge railways, along with stations, rolling stock and disused railway land, entered into Government ownership. For the next fifty two years this all belonged to the people (you and me) including the debts incurred during its total operation.

In 1996, all this came to an abrupt end when, in the twilight months of John Major's reign as Prime Minister before the May 1997 election, the privatisation of British Railways was rushed through the statute books.

This Act split the rail network into two basic components namely Railtrack which became responsible for all track and signaling, while rolling stock and station upkeep and development was franchised to many private companies some of whom operated as bus companies! New ticket pricing structures appeared with some companies competing with others on the same routes.

The new structure resulted in a chaotic fares' system, but this competitive edge did not occur at St. Neots because the station was maintained by the same company, WAGN (West Anglian Great Northern).

Changes at St. Neots Station in 2008-09

The approach scene at St. Neots Station has changed for good. This has been precipitated by the rapid growth of the town plus the spawning of the new town called Cambourne, a mere 3 miles west of Cambridge.

Although St. Neots commuters find various means, other than the car, of reaching the station, Cambourne commuters, to points south of Hitchin, have discovered that using St. Neots Station, rather than Cambridge with all its attendant city rush-hour hassle, is so much better.

This has put such an enormous amount of pressure on the current station parking facilities surrounding residential streets have been blighted by lines of roadside cars.

Network Rail have decided to extend the station's parking area with an extra 150 parking spaces by demolishing the 'South' goods shed and weighbridge complex. This was completed in the autumn of 2009 but, due to swingeing daily parking fees, complaints still emanate from the

Fig 79 – South-west view of the old South Goods Shed from Platform 3 during Dec. 2008 demolition. (Source – author)

Fig 80 – South Goods Yard 1850 weighbridge office prior to demolition in December 2008. The plastic pipes were ready for installation in the replacement car park extension built in 2009 in the vain hope of relieving off-street parking. (Source – author)

surrounding residents. The shed was used as a furniture sales depot after BR stopped its parcels delivery service in the 1980s.

Since the furniture dealer died 4 years ago, the shed had been derelict. Slates had fallen off the roof and the loading doors' canopy had begun to disintegrate. The latter structure was encased, in its last months, in scaffolding to protect passing station-bound road traffic.

The weighbridge complex was composed of a small office which had been occupied by a taxi firm until November 2008. Inside was the complete and original WH Pooley weighing equipment while outside was the weighing platform supplied by the same firm. The taxi firm was relocated to a portacabin at the 'North' end of the station's main building so that demolition work could start in mid-December 2008 (weighbridge) and late-2009 (goods shed).

According to the detail on an 1898 photograph, the weighbridge office was already in place suggesting it was an original building from the grand opening of the line in August 1850. The goods shed may well have been of the same era.

Tornado 'hits' homes in St. Neots and Eaton Socon

The incredible story surrounding the dream of the magnificent beast of the steam engine "Tornado" epitomises the fact that, although Britain was once the innovative workhorse of the world, there is still life in the 'old dog of a nation' yet.

A fanatical bunch of railway engineers, young and old, joined together on the 7th April 1990 at Darlington (where this book's story began) and dreamt of the day when a totally extinct class of steam locomotive would be built from scratch by their voluntary efforts and zeal.

The Class was initiated by Sir Nigel Gresley before he died in 1941 and, with the Second World War and 1948 nationalisation intervening, the stewardship of this superb steam engine's final modified design fell upon the shoulders of Arthur Peppercorn OBE in 1946 when he was entrusted with L. & N.E.R.'s role as chief mechanical engineer (CME).

Arthur was not satisfied with the design of the Class A1 engine and set about the task of introducing his own innovative ideas into the engineering. The first engine of the Class A2 to emerge from the Doncaster Works sporting his modifications was named "A H Peppercorn", the only one during L. & N.E.R. ownership before nationalisation, and the last rolled out of the works in August 1948. These engines were often described as 'the best express passenger engines to grace this country's rails' doing efficient economical work between Glasgow, Edinburgh and King's Cross. In their first twelve years they clocked up an average of 4.8 million miles.

The last main line steam locomotive was built at Swindon and brought into commission on the 24th March 1960, namely a 9F bulk cargo engine and aptly named "Evening Star". It had been decided by British Railways, in the early 1950s, to

change from steam to diesel and electric engines. The Peppercorn Class A1 would have a working life until the mid-1960s when all were withdrawn and sent to the scrapheap. Not one out of the 49 survived the blowtorch. How did the idea germinate to build Peppercorn "Tornado", and what is the connection with St. Neots and its station?

It took eighteen years and £3 million for the idea to come to fruition in Darlington's railway works after Gresley's Peppercorn's A1 plans had been discovered in the Doncaster works design department. A bunch of fanatical railway enthusiasts gathered together in Darlington in 1990 and spawned the 'crazy' idea to build a working A1 Class specimen. After eighteen years of back-breaking work the engine finally rolled out of the works for the first

Fig 81 – 'Tornado' in February 2009 on its inaugural run to King's Cross before the addition and of its nameplate in York a few days later. The engine is adjacent to the old North Signal-box site.
(Courtesy of Ian Hornsby)

time, and passed all the stringent tests to be let loose on the national railway network.

One of the engine's first trips, before its nameplate was attached and unveiled in York by Prince Charles a few days later, was to King's Cross via St. Neots. It was on a snow-covered sun-drenched cloudless Saturday morning in February 2009 when hundreds of lineside spectators gathered at the station in anticipation of the arrival of "Tornado". Eventually, the white plume of smoky steam appeared on the northern horizon.

The train was due to pass through at about 70 mph but it had slowed down to change lines a mile to the north to allow a scheduled electric express to overtake it at twice the speed. "Tornado" was only coasting through at 45 mph; what a bonus for the gathered, and a photo-shooting opportunity! It was almost as if it knew of its connection with the station!

What is this connection? Arthur Peppercorn was born at Stoke Prior, Leominster, Herefordshire in 1889, the son of the vicar Alfred Peppercorn. Alfred was born in Eaton Socon, today's western suburb 1.5 miles from St. Neots centre! He was the son of Mr. William Peppercorn junior who was the son of the land and rent agent for the Earl of Sandwich mentioned on page one of this book. You may remember the Earl was a major property owner in St. Neots in the 1840s and Colonel William Peppercorn was the father of William Peppercorn junior, lawyer and original business partner of Octavius Wilkinson (which takes you back to the start of this book).

Col. William Peppercorn, senior owned Manor Farm, now a housing estate and just a few metres south of Cambridge Road, St. Neots (and 200 metres from the

station). Neighbouring Shortsands House, built around 1820, became vacant and the Colonel bought it before dying in 1833. W Peppercorn, junior bought, and went to live at, the Cock Inn in 1845 next door to the village church and only one hundred metres from his university friend and business partner Octavius Wilkinson. William renamed the Cock Inn as the "Manor House", which stayed in the family's possession until 1923 (and demolished in 1965).

Fig 82 – Arthur Peppercorn
(Courtesy of Peter Hall)

The "Manor House" was where William Peppercorn's son, Alfred was born in 1852 before following his father to Cambridge University and entering the church, initially as a curate, at Woodhay, Hampshire. After being transferred to Stoke Prior, Leominster, Herefordshire Arthur was born one of seventeen children, no less! Alfred wanted Arthur to follow in his footsteps to become a vicar and enter the church (I am surprised he knew who he was!),

How did Arthur Peppercorn's interest in steam engines develop? His widow, a still very active Mrs. Mather, told me: "Arthur's father one day telephoned the private school he attended to ask if he could take his son out for a few hours. Arthur's father, some time during that visit, had asked his son if he had yet decided what career path to follow; was it to be a vicar, like himself, or a doctor? Arthur's response was that he wanted to be an engine driver! The rest is history".

The next time you hear about, or see, the "Tornado", this connection with St. Neots and Eaton Socon might spring to your thoughts.

Fig 83 – Shortsands House, family home of the Peppercorns, in Cambridge Road St. Neots pre-1845. (now the Bethany Nursing Home).
(Courtesy of Paul Todd)

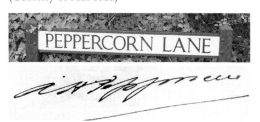

Fig 84 – Peppercorn Lane, Eaton Socon street nameplate and Arthur Peppercorn's signature.
(Source – author)

The Future

St. Neots Station's future appears to be secure with the town's role in life changing from one processing agricultural products and industrial units to a bustling urban centre that has grown by 700 per cent in the last half century. New housing estates continue to be built, such as Love's Farm, and the planned 5,000 dwellings site to the south, both being adjacent to the station.

The town's function has changed dramatically to one which supports a workforce centred on five industrial estates, but many of whose people travel to other places to ply their trade thus turning it into a commuter town. The town's station has played a considerable influence in this metamorphosis with the electrification of the line. The goods yards have long disappeared to be replaced by commuter car parks.

The 1875 Channel Tunnel dream finally became a reality and was opened over a century later, in 1996, and is now a well-established fact-of-life. Two of the trains used on that route came out of mothballs, were rented by GNER and sped through the station from King's Cross to York. Now that St. Pancras is the new Tunnel terminus in London, and being adjacent to King's Cross, it should be easy to build a spur rail line from the former station to link in to the line to St. Neots. Will this be built and will Channel Tunnel trains be seen once more through the station?

St. Neots Station is thriving once more. So much so that, at the latest set of figures published by the Office of Rail Regulation for 2008/09, the station had a grand total of 1,036,380 passengers arriving and concluding their journeys on its platforms. This was a staggering five per cent increase

Fig 85 – Channel Tunnel train speeding through Huntingdon Station from St. Neots in 2008 while on temporary two-year contract to GNER. (Courtesy of Allan Mott)

on the previous year. The footbridge is so busy at rush hours, there are queues several deep waiting to ascend the steps from the platforms.

It is rumoured that plans are in the design stage for a new extended footbridge, with lifts for disabled access (at present totally denied), more car parking on the Cambridge side of the tracks and an extra eleven trains each week. Already, First Capital Direct,

the company now dealing with local passenger traffic, added an extra 5,500 seats in May 2010. All this makes nonsense of Mr. Huskisson's gloom-and-doom statements fifty years ago to journalists. If projected building plans go ahead after the current recession ends, the station will find itself in the middle of two commuter estates of over six thousand houses as well as serving the rest of St. Neots.

Chapter Six
Joe Doncaster's photography
of trains and locomotives at St Neots

LNER Pacific Class A4 no. 60025 'Falcon'. Midday King's Cross–Peterborough return service c.1960.

Class A4 No.60017 'Silver Fox' This locomotive was shedded at King's Cross. One of four locomotives used on the pre-war 'Silver Jubilee' train service, the others being "Silver Link", "Quicksilver", and "Silver King".

This train is double-headed by two Atlantic 4-4-2 engines, G.N.R. Class C1 no. 990 "Henry Oakley" and C2 no. 251, on Sept 20th 1953 to commemorate the centenary of Doncaster Loco Works. The train is at the north end of the North goods yard. Designed by Henry Ivatt in 1897, a total of 22 C1s were built from 1898-1903 at Doncaster. The second engine, C2 Class no. "251", was the evolved larger boiler design with 94 built at Doncaster between 1902 and 1910.

LNER Peppercorn A1 Class 'Silurian' No. 60121 pausing at St. Neots Station 1960.

Class A3 no. 60044 'Melton' adjacent to North goods yard warehouse and granary.

Class A1 No.60114 "W.P. Allen" – This class was a Peppercorn development of Thompson Class A1/1.

Class J3 E4117 - had been re-numbered 4117 on 2 June 1946 from 4100. The E suffix was added as an identifier to a few Eastern Region locomotives in early 1948 at the beginning of BR ownership. The locomotive was shedded at Hitchin and withdrawn in June 1952.

Class J6 No.64175 - A Hitchin locomotive. A standard LNER 'Toad D' 20 ton brake van is behind the tender.

Ex-L& NER Class A3 4-6-2 No.60059 "Tracery".

Peppercorn Class A2 No.60533 "Happy Knight" - a Gresley coach attached.

Thompson LNER Class B1 no. 61168 was an example of the class used for mixed traffic work, and was LNER's equivalent to the highly successful LMS 'Black 5' type. This photo shows an empty coal train heading north just south of the station to Peterborough's New England shunting yard in the 1950s.

LMS Pacific no. 46245 'City of London'. Possibly on what was known as the Exchanges where engines from 1948 nationalised companies were tested for suitability on new regional lines. This engine usually ran from Euston to Glasgow on the West Coast Main Line.

Double-header Midland Railway (MR) Compound no. 1000 and LNER Class B12 2-6-0 No. 61572 south of St. Neots pulling a 'special' northbound in the 1960s.

Great Western Railway no. 7029 'Clun Castle' special northbound at the north end of the station c.1968.

British Railways (BR) Britannia Class no. 70020 'Mercury'. "Home Counties Railway Society" excursion c.1968.

B.R. Deltic no. D9018 'Ballymoss' (renumbered 55018) scrapped on October 12th 1981.

Final prototype version of B.R.'s Co-Co Napier named 'Deltic' (no. 1) heading for King's Cross in winter c.1957 with iconic gull-wing motif on the front. The engine is now preserved at Shildon Railway Museum, Co. Durham (annexe of NRM, York). At the time, it was the most powerful diesel engine in the world; built by English Electric, Preston. Only 21 were built for use on the East Coast Main Line from 1961–81. They were powered by two Napier 'Deltic' 18-cylinder engines contributing to a total engine weight of 99 tons.

Brush No. D 0280 "Falcon" Type 4 2,700 bhp diesel-electric - This was iftted with two Maybach V-type engines. This train was London-bound.

BR Type 4 'Peak' 2,500 bhp diesel-electric no. D 168.

Pullmam Express with diesel 'Lion' heading south in September 1963. 'Lion' remained in (testing) service for only 18 months before withdrawal. It has often been described as the forerunner of the Class 47 diesels so ubiquitously used all over the U.K. thereafter.

Preserved LNER Class A3 No.4472 "Flying Scotsman" on an Ian Allan Railtours 'special' in c.1965.

P23 – B.R. Standard 4-6-2 Class 7MT No. 70000 'Britannia' built 1951 passing St. Neots South Goods Yard in the evening on a return to Grimsby via the East Lincs. line, with empty fish vans – c1960-66.

Ministry of Supply War Dept. Class 8F 2–8–0 No. 90744 with an 'Up' coal train from Tyneside just south of 'Rowley's Bridge' (Priory Hill Br.), St. Neots. The palatial Stationmaster's House is in the background and built during the 1898 widening scheme. The train was probably heading for London with a type of coal for a specific power station in London.

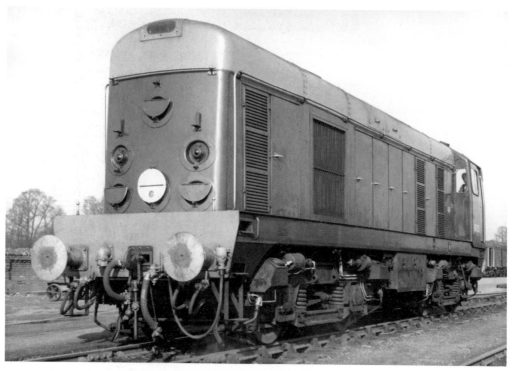

Unidentified 1,000 b.h.p. English Electric Type 1 Class 20 (Bo-Bo) diesel-electric locomotive, which replaced the steam engine for servicing the goods yards.

B.R. Standard Class 9F 2-10-0 No. 92037 – designed at Brighton for heavy freight haulage, but could serve equally well as a passenger locomotive. This engine was based at New England (Peterborough) when this photograph was taken by Joe Doncaster.

Austerity Class no. 90256 from a Riddles Ministry of Supply design in 1942 seen here shunting in the South goods yard. It was a regular Peterborough New England-based locomotive.

Opposite page: The 'Old and the New' – a new (1958) 2,000 b.h.p. English Electric Class 40 diesel-electric, No. D206 awaits a change-over to the 'Flying Scotsman' express train at King's Cross from the just arrived Gresley Class A3 No. 60075 'St. Frusquin' (Gateshead Shed) which also bears the 'Flying Scotsman' headboard. The latter was built in 1924, rebuilt in 1942 and withdrawn in 1964.

Above: Booth Concrete Co's. bridge beams, cast on the work's site adjacent to North goods yard, being dispatched on southbound 'slow' line at the south end of the station.

Left: A Ferranti transformer in the South goods yard destined for Little Barford Power Station c.1955.

Index

BIBLIOGRAPHY

Our Iron Roads – F S Williams

History of the North Eastern Railway – J J Tomlinson 1912

The Comic Bradshaw or Bubbles from the Boiler – A R Peach

Railway Age in Bedfordshire – F G Cockman 1974

The History of the Gt. Northern Railway – C H Grinling